For Cal and Carolyn Halcombe —
I treasure

[signature]

Funny Bone

Amusing stories short and sassy

Hatcher Crenshaw

Five Star Press   Richmond

Funny Bone

Amusing stories – short and sassy

By Hatcher Crenshaw

Published by:

Five Star Press
Post Office Box 8454
Richmond, VA 23226

All rights reserved. No part of this book may be reproduced or transmitted in any form or by any means, electronic or mechanical, including photocopying, recording or by any information storage and retrieval system without written permission from the author, except for the inclusion of brief quotations in a review.

Copyright © 2000 by Hatcher Crenshaw

Printed in the United States of America

This book is a collection of stories which happened to the author and his friends. Some of the names of the characters have been changed for various reasons. Any resemblance of the fictitious names to real persons, living or dead, is coincidental and not intended by the author.

Library of Congress Catalog Card Number 99-095305

ISBN 0-9673102-0-2

Dedication

For Mary Spotswood

and the MEWS gang

Acknowledgments

The author acknowledges with grateful thanks and sincere appreciation to the following individuals:

James A. "Jerry" Jerritt, my editor, for his encouragement, support and expertise.

Ruth Curtis for her superb technical help and perseverance in seeing this project through to the very end.

Spot Crenshaw for her wonderful artwork, the delightful illustrations and graphics.

And to the non-family fine folks who were the driving forces for my inspiration and motivation (alphabetically):

Lois Amidon, Dave and Sally Beverly, Clifford and Anne Bussells, Fred Carr, Frank Giles, Malcolm McNeill, Martha Moore, Ottie Moore, Frank and Betty Payne, Bill Singleton, Peg and the late Arthur Spangenthal and the past and present walkers at Willow Lawn.

Contents

Herbert's Car	11
Making the Deal	19
Jacques' Faux Pas	27
The Royal Visit	33
Duke's Day	41
High School Reunion	47
Twirling Tassels	53
Handsome Harry	61
Versailles Excursion	67
Square Piano	75
Doctor's Exchange	81
Lopez	87
Cud'n Gillette	95
The Ultimate Put-down	101
Magic Pills	107

Birthday Girl	**111**
Mama's Politics	**115**
Buck & Sally	**121**
Sunny Eyes	**127**
Sweet and Sour	**133**
American Mother	**139**
Football Dilemma	**147**
Value of Dollar	**155**
Mall Walk	**161**
Jack, the Boss	**165**
Sun Roof	**169**
Pen Set	**173**
Sheriff	**179**
You Can't Win	**185**

Funny Bone...

The place at the back of the elbow where the ulnar nerve rests against a prominence of the humerus.

or

A sense of humor

By permission. From Merriam-Webster's
Collegiatte ®Dictionary, 10th Edition
©1999 by Merriam-Webster, Incorporated

Herbert's Car

When a minister in the Episcopal Church leaves his position for another assignment or retirement, it takes approximately one year to find a replacement. During that twelve-month period, the members of the congregation have to rely on visiting preachers, seminary students, or retired members of the clergy to conduct Sunday services.

Applicant priests are also invited to visit the church and be tested in the pulpit with their own sermons as well as to be interviewed for the available opening.

Such was the case at Richard Hunt's Episcopal Church where he was a member of the vestry and Treasurer. Their present minister had resigned to take a position at a much larger church in another state. The leadership had hired a retired clergyman as an interim pastor for one year. In that way, it would give the church adequate time to make a final decision on a replacement.

The former rector had an agreement that allowed him to use his own personal automobile for conducting church business for which he was reimbursed for his operating expenses. It was good for him as well as beneficial to the church. There had been no obligation to provide another vehicle for his use.

The vestry committee had decided to lease a car for one year for the interim preacher, but when Richard found out the cost of renting, he suggested they purchase a good, dependable used car. He felt that it would cost more than five thousand dollars to lease for a year, but much less to purchase and then sell when the interim left. He was asked to investigate the car market with the understanding that the purchase price be limited to $5,000, preferably less. Since they did not want to prolong their decision, he was asked to make a recommendation to them within two weeks.

Herbert's Car

Richard checked the used car lots and the advertisements in the newspaper and made a few telephone calls. He was primarily interested in the age and condition of the vehicle with particular attention to its mileage. Other salient features were important not only for the church's use, but also for its marketability when it would be offered for sale in one year. The asking price was important as well as the primary reason for selling.

After eliminating most offerings for one reason or another, Richard decided on a three-year old, four door Dodge sedan that had been driven fourteen thousand miles. It had been owned by a retired gentleman who had passed away. His widow had her own Oldsmobile, and she had married a widower who had his own Cadillac and a sporty convertible that his deceased first wife had driven, so the couple had four automobiles between them. Richard thought that this was good enough reason for them to sell. He also liked the fact that they were older adults and were more than likely to have serviced the cars systematically.

He went to meet with the couple, Charles and Matilda Jackson, and to see the Dodge. It had a beautiful maroon finish and was in great condition. Mrs. Jackson was asking $4,200 for it. In the early 1980's, this was a very reasonable price.

Richard figured that the new minister would drive it no more than 1,000 miles a month. After using it for a year, it should have around 26,000 miles on the odometer and would probably sell for $3,000 or more. Then it would be four years old. That would be a good deal for the church, costing a great deal less than the rental payments and at a decent price which was under his budget of $5,000.

Richard explained to the couple that he was buying on behalf of his church for a new pastor. He had to check with the vestry committee before he could make a valid offer. It was up to them to give their final approval for the purchase.

An appointment was made for him to return the next afternoon.

During the evening, each member of the committee was contacted by telephone and told about the vehicle. Everyone was delighted and authorized the purchase of it for $4,200. Two members made suggestions emphasizing that the church was the purchaser and that there could be some tax benefits to the sellers. One person suggested that if the car were donated to the church, the gift would be 100% tax deductible to the donor. Richard was asked to explain the tax advantages to the couple.

Driving to his appointment the next afternoon, Richard thought about his various conversations and suggestions from the night before. It wasn't going to be easy.

Herbert's Car

He knew it was important to get Mr. Jackson to approve of his wife donating the car to the church. If not an outright gift, then maybe at a lower price. Richard figured that Mr. Jackson would be a key player in the negotiations. It was important to get him to go along with whatever his wife wanted to do.

He met with the couple.

Mrs. Jackson met him at the door and invited him in. Mr. Jackson was sitting in an easy chair watching television. He was dressed in khaki trousers and his undershirt, and drinking a can of beer. He nodded at his wife and Richard.

Richard began, "Mrs. Jackson, you know that I am here on behalf of my church. We want your car and we need it.. If you make a donation of the car to the church which is a charitable organization, you could get a 100% deduction on your income tax. I just wanted you to understand all options that are opened for you."

"It's not my car," she responded. "Not really. It belonged to my first husband, Herbert. I don't think I could give it away."

Mr. Jackson had not turned off the television set and it was difficult to hear what his wife was saying.

Richard frowned, "It's hard to hear you with the noise from the television."

Mrs. Jackson turned to her husband and said,

"Charlie, please turn the television off. We can't hear what we're saying."

Charlie turned the sound down a bit and asked, "Is this better? I'm real interested in seeing the ending to this program."

Both Richard and Mrs. Jackson nodded that it was better.

Continuing, Mrs. Jackson said, "It's a little better, but turn it off when the program's over."

Charlie waved his hand and shook his head up and down in agreement.

Mrs. Jackson looked back at Richard and repeated that it was her first husband's car and that she could not give it away. It never crossed her mind to donate it to a charity.

Mr. Jackson interrupted, "Herbert would turn over in his grave. I don't think he ever set foot in a church after he was 12 years old."

"Hush, Charlie. Have some respect for the dead," Mrs. Jackson retorted.

"I ain't disrespecting the dead, Tillie. I'm just stating a fact. Herbert never took you to church, did he?"

Matilda Jackson frowned, "I don't think that this gentleman," as she pointed to Richard, "wants to hear about Herbert's going or not going to church."

She looked at Richard, waiting for a response.

Richard smiled, "You're right, Mrs. Jackson.

Herbert's Car

Your husband's doings were his own. It's not up to me to make any comment."

Matilda shook her head approvingly.

Richard continued, "I just wanted you to know about gifts to the church."

"Charlie," Mrs. Jackson said, "I'd like to do something nice in memory of Herbert. He was a good man. After all, we were married for 42 wonderful years."

Charlie leaned forward in his chair, saying, "Oh, I know, Tillie. I know. But Herbert ain't here to know. If you want to do something for him, why don't you sell the car to the church for $3,500. That way, you'll get some money which you surely deserve and at the same time, you'll be honoring and remembering Herbert in a very nice way."

Mrs. Jackson thought for a moment, smiling, "Oh, that's just great, Charlie. You never cease to amaze me, always coming up with the right answers."

A happy Matilda Jackson beamed at Richard. Then, her expression changed to serious as she tilted her head back and looked up at the ceiling.

She spoke. "I hope you approve, dear. I'm selling your car to the church for $3,000."

Richard thought that she wasn't looking at the ceiling, but gazing up to heaven. She was talking to Herbert.

She kept conversing with her dead husband, "I feel like I'm giving something for you, Herbert. I know the car is worth more, but it's for a good cause. It's a church, Herbert. An Episcopal Church."

Matilda smiled and looked at Richard and Charlie.

Richard smiled back at her.

Charlie took another sip from his beer can and grunted.

Making the Deal

The real estate firm in Richmond, Virginia where I worked as a salesman specialized in selling, leasing and managing commercial and industrial properties - office buildings, shopping centers, warehouses and other industrial buildings. It was an all-out involvement in commerce and industry.

I had been assigned to solve a specific problem at a medium sized shopping center. There was

Funny Bone

adequate parking in front of the stores for customers and employees, but not much space in the rear, where trucks tried to maneuver in and out for loading and unloading. Sometimes, it was impossible for more than one vehicle to move around, and the storeowners were concerned about the inefficient and slow manner in which they received their goods. After all, this was their livelihood; buying at wholesale and selling at retail. Something had to be done to alleviate the situation.

Adjoining the shopping center in the rear was a strip of land that would widen the passageway and even provide extra parking. There was no building on it. It was a natural solution to solve our problem.

After checking it out, I found that the land was approximately seventy feet wide and ran all the way with our property line plus an additional fifty feet. The owner was listed as Martha Harrison and the real estate tax bill was sent to her at an address in Omaha, Nebraska.

After looking in the telephone directory to see if she was listed locally, which she wasn't, I wrote her a letter, explaining that we represented the adjacent property and were interested in purchasing her land. Several days later, she replied that she would be very interested in selling, but that she understood there were ruins of former

Confederate trenches and fortifications on the property. Under those circumstances, she was reluctant to do anything until it could be substantiated that it was not of any historical importance. She had a first cousin who was a retired teacher in Richmond. She was notifying him to look into the situation and had given him my name to contact. He had been familiar with the property through the years.

I telephoned Mrs. Harrison, telling her that I would investigate the history of the land so that I would have some information on it before her cousin contacted me. County records, the State library, the historical association and numerous Civil War groups were available as well as area individual history experts.

In my initial conversation with her cousin, he informed me that he recently had verified several reliable sources and had come to the conclusion that the tract was of no historical significance. It was only an old rumor he had heard most of his life that it had been a Civil War entrenchment.

After I had made some more inquiries, the cousin and I met. He showed me several documents he had kept over the years relating to the property. The consensus was that the land could be sold. It never had been a Confederate milestone. He thought that his cousin was foolish to continue to keep it, particularly since she lived so far away. He would encourage her to sell.

As a matter of fact, part of the land was a narrow ditch that was about one hundred feet long. It was filled with broken bottles, empty drink cans, old automobile tires and other trashed paraphernalia, overgrown, unkempt and looked awful.

When I called Mrs. Harrison in Omaha and told her of our findings, she said that she thought she had better not sell it. She told me that when she lived in Richmond, which was most of her life, she had heard that the property was an important Civil War landmark. She paid no attention to her cousin's findings or his recommendation. Nothing could convince her to sell. She thanked me for my interest in it and would contact me further if she changed her mind

Change her mind she did.

Over the next several months we had countless telephone conversations. First, she thought she would sell, then decided overnight not to sell. She thought it was the wrong thing to do. It went back and forth many times.

Sell. Not sell. Sell. Not sell.

She had no idea how it looked today, only remembering what it was like many years ago. It was ridiculous for her to continue to pay the real estate taxes on it with no present or future potential.

I was getting exasperated. I even woke up in the

Making the Deal

middle of the night thinking about it. Maybe she needed a push. She was a long way from Virginia and could not visualize what it was like. I went out to the property and took a series of photographs which I sent to her to see. They didn't faze her at all.

I decided to travel to Omaha and visit her in person. If I called before leaving, she would probably tell me not to waste my time and money and to stay at home. I concluded that an unannounced trip was in order. A final decision had to be made regarding the property. It had gone on much too long. My real estate firm still wanted the land and was impatient, not knowing which way to turn. The merchants in the shopping center were not too happy and couldn't understand our situation. It was very annoying to me, too.

I flew to Omaha.

After settling in at my hotel, I took a taxi to Mrs. Harrison's apartment building. She lived in a modern high-rise structure close to a large beautiful park. The receptionist asked if I was expected. Upon hearing my story, she welcomed me and suggested that I sit in the waiting area of the lobby. Since Mrs. Harrison was not expected to return home for two more hours, I decided to take a short walk and see the sights in the neighborhood.

On the flight out, I thought about how I should

approach her. During my walk, I honed in on my plan. It was all worked out in my mind. I was determined to take the bull by its horns and either make the deal right then and there or return home and forget about it forever.

About an hour later, I returned to the apartment building and talked for awhile with the receptionist. She informed me that Mrs. Harrison had been a widow for five years, had no children and was the manager of an upscale woman's specialty store. She had moved into the building four years ago and was liked by everyone there.

A short time later, I was interrupted from my magazine reading by an attractive middle aged lady, impeccably dressed.

"I'm Martha Harrison. I understand you have been waiting to see me."

I jumped up. As I looked at her, I thought to myself, "She sure doesn't look the way she sounds on the telephone." I was expecting to see an average woman on the young side of sixty-five, a little overweight, not too stylish and with solid gray hair. I was dead wrong. She looked like someone from an advertisement in a magazine, not one of those thin, emaciated young beautiful things. She looked great and had the air of a professional businesswoman. And not a gray hair on her head.

I introduced myself.

Making the Deal

"What are you doing here in Omaha?"

"I came out to see you about your property in Richmond."

She appeared concerned. "I thought we had finalized that on the telephone."

I replied, "I never realized that you had made a final decision. I just had to come out here, look you in the eye, and hear you say that you are or are not going to sell. Let's resolve this once and for all."

I stared at her and continued, "This game of ours has been going on much too long. It's beyond being exasperating. I can't take it anymore. If you say you will sell, then my trip out here will not have been in vain. But, if you say you will not sell, than I'll go back home and forget it. And you'll never hear from me again. I've got to know without a doubt whether you will or you won't. And that's what I'm all about."

I hope that I hadn't come on too strong. But, this was my last and final effort to get her to sell. I didn't want to make her angry and ruin my chances in the very beginning. I just stood there, waiting for her response.

She looked at me and broke out in the biggest grin.

"Oh, honey, it's so good to hear a Virginia accent again. It's been such a long time."

I grinned back at her.

Funny Bone

Continuing, she suggested, "Let's go up to my apartment and talk about this calmly over a bourbon and water."

She paused a moment, then asked, "I should have asked. You do drink bourbon and water, don't you?"

Responding in my best southern accent, I drawled, "Why, Miz Harrison, ma'am, Ah wuz raised on bourbon 'n branch watah."

Early the next afternoon, I walked with a snappy step from my hotel to meet Mrs. Harrison at her attorney's office. An option to purchase her Richmond property was drawn up and duly signed by all parties.

Ah want y'all to know this. Ah jes love Omaha. Sho nuff.

Jacques' Faux Pas

Bert and Vickie sold their beloved large home where they had lived for many years. Both of their two daughters were living on their own, so the empty nesters decided to move into a smaller place for themselves. They looked around at houses and apartments for several months and finally decided to purchase an ideal two-bedroom townhouse condominium.

Funny Bone

It is not easy to downsize your home. After all, a great number of hours each day is spent there, more so than any other place. It was a hard decision for Bert and Vickie to make and they were relieved when it was done. They were happy that their search was over, and that they had found exactly what they wanted.

The new residence was perfect for two people. You entered an entrance hall that led to a spacious living room with large sliding glass doors that overlooked a patio which was enclosed with an attractive natural wood privacy fence. It made the space bright and spacious. They had a medium rose-colored awning installed outside over the door opening which gave a warm, healthy glow to the room during the day. The kitchen and dining area were off the entrance hall in the front, and a half bath was located under the stairway to the second floor.

Upstairs were a bathroom and two bedrooms, one facing the front, the other, the rear. There was also a linen closet and an extra large storage area off the hall.

The fashionably located property contained over two hundred living units with an abundance of parking spaces and a swimming pool. It had been a very successful apartment venture before being turned into condos. It was extremely popular with the public. Demand for the property was high and

Jacques' Faux Pas

the rising sales prices demonstrated its popularity.

Bert and Vickie knew several friends and acquaintances that had moved there. All were pleased with their neighbors and were well satisfied with the management team. They were delighted with their decision and were looking forward to living there.

When the couple moved into their new home, they completely redecorated it to their own taste. They had inherited several family portraits which they were planning to hang in the living room, where they had installed several hidden electric plugs in the wall for the individual portrait lights. There were no unsightly electric cords running up the wall from the floor. I was impressed with that.

Their home was beautifully furnished with many antiques and art objects, including several of Vickie's own works of sculpture. Both had worked hard to make it enjoyable to live in as well as to express their own aesthetic feelings. The tasteful décor reflected what was known as Virginia Classic, a style which emanated from the early English plantation houses along the James River. It fit well with the colonial style architecture of the buildings and the adjoining landscape.

_ One day after living there for about a year, Bert and Vickie received a telephone call from a friend named Blanche. She told them about a friend of hers who was an antiques and art dealer and was moving to Richmond. She had met him a few years back in New York City and had bought several items from him there. They had become good friends.

Bert and Vickie had heard of him. It was rumored that he originally came from France. His name was Jacques and everyone who met him was charmed with his captivating European accent. The word was out in the community that with his credentials he should be an outstanding business success.

Blanche was helping Jacques with his move and giving him support in getting settled. It was a fun thing for her and she was enjoying it immensely. They had driven through the neighborhood but did not go into any of the properties. Jacques had liked what he had seen of the outside and was very interested in seeing one of the units on the inside. Blanche wanted to know if she could bring him over to inspect their townhouse.

Bert and Vickie were thrilled to think that Jacques himself wanted to look at their home rather than anyone else's. There were several units advertised for rent and for sale, but he wanted to see theirs. They wondered what he would think after he had seen it.

The important visit was confirmed for Thursday at three thirty in the afternoon. Vickie thought that this would be wonderful since it was just about tea time. She decided to go all out with her silver tea service that had belonged to her maternal grandmother. It was elegant and had her own family coat of arms engraved in the middle of the tray and on both the coffee and teapots. She was very proud of it and liked to use it on special occasions.. It was very regal looking and always garnered many oohs and ahs from her guests.

She remembered the time she and Bert had afternoon tea at the Ritz in London and how delighted and surprised the waiters were when they found out that their names, Vickie and Bert, were actually Victoria and Albert. Those names, their former queen and her prince consort, were still held in the highest regard by all after so many years.

Vickie thought she would emulate that wonderful English ritual. She would make a few open faced cucumber sandwiches and bake some scones to be served with strawberry jam and clotted cream. She wanted to do it just like the British did.

Vickie tried to contact Blanche to let her know that she and Jacques were invited to stay for afternoon tea when they came to inspect the property, but she was unable to reach her after several telephone calls. She was disappointed that Blanche didn't have an answering machine.

Funny Bone

Before noon on Thursday, Blanche called and canceled the afternoon meeting, explaining that Jacques had bought a condo at another location. She hoped that she had not put them to too much trouble and was sorry to have to cancel at such a late hour.

Bert and Vickie were really disappointed. They had made every effort to have their place looking great and in perfect condition to show as well as preparing the tea party.

On the telephone, Vickie said, "Oh, I'm so sorry. We both were anxious to meet Jacques and were hoping that he would buy a unit near us. We were so happy that he wanted to live in our neighborhood."

"It wasn't for him," Blanche responded. "He already bought a house for himself."

She paused a moment before continuing, "This was to be for his houseboy."

The Royal Visit

Joe Fallon always liked to cook. Even as a small boy, he was fascinated watching his mother prepare supper in the evening. He especially liked the big holiday affairs when all the relatives came to the Fallon home and the kitchen was busy and exciting. He was thrilled when he was putting the water glasses on the table or taking out the trash. It wasn't cooking, but it was a necessary part of the kitchen duties.

When he reached his teenage years, Joe had

become a moderately good cook. His mother had taught him the basic fundamentals and had let him prepare family meals all by himself. He read many books and magazines on the art of cooking and had worked in the kitchen at a boys summer camp for three years.while he was still in high school. By the time he finished school, he had made up his mind that he wanted to be involved in the food business.

When Joe joined the Navy, he was sent to cooking school and became a first class Navy cook. He was assigned to a ship for several months until a high ranking officer discovered his talent and took him to a naval club in the Washington, DC area. The officer had been transferred there and thought that Joe would be a big asset to the club. He remained there until his enlistment was completed and then returned to civilian life. He enrolled in a culinary arts school and later became a certified chef.

His first job was in an upscale restaurant. He was very happy working there, but became disenchanted when he learned that the business was being sold. The owner had offered it to some of the other employees. Joe was not included in the deal. A few of the buyers had not worked at the restaurant as long as he had. Since he was not treated fairly, he decided to accept a standing offer from a private club. Some of the members were

The Royal Visit

former Navy acquaintances and knew of Joe's talent and capabilities. They were very pleased that he made the decision to work for the club.

During his years there, Joe fell in love with a young lady he had met on a blind date. They went together for two years before they married. His wife always claimed that she married him because he was such a good cook.

She boasted, "I may be the chief bottle washer in the family, but Joe is definitely the cook."

Later on, Joe was offered a position as chef at a foreign embassy in Washington, where the salary was much greater than what he was making. The offer could not have come at a better time as his wife was pregnant with their first child. Even though he was happy at the club, the embassy position was something that he could not turn down.

After several months in his new job, Joe was made Acting Master Chef while the regular Master Chef took an extended vacation to go back to his home in Europe. Joe did a great job. Many of the kitchen staff were European natives, but they managed to communicate with one another, sometimes in English, sometimes in their native tongues and occasionally in sign language.

One afternoon while Joe was in charge, the ambassador summoned him to his office. His Excellency was very elated because two members of his country's royal family would be visiting Washington the following month. He wanted to alert Joe that an important party was being planned and that Joe would be in charge of the food and drinks. The details would be forthcoming from the staff in charge. Any recommendations or guidance from Joe would be appreciated during the planning stage.

In the following weeks, Joe was involved with the group in charge, giving advice, making suggestions, and working on the menu regarding the food and drinks.

The entire embassy staff was excited over the pending royal visit. Joe had designated an energetic baker in the kitchen named Orlando to be his number one assistant. Since additional waiters would be needed for the function, Orlando had recommended some very dependable friends who had moved recently to Washington from a South American country. Orlando spoke the language and assured everyone that they would be perfect. They were working part-time for a well-known beltway caterer and were experienced with the local party scene. They had worked at several big embassy parties in the area and had been highly recommended. Orlando was authorized to hire five of them for the special affair.

Royal Day finally arrived. The embassy was at fever pitch. Everyone was busy making last

The Royal Visit

minute adjustments to every facet of the building. Flowers were placed every where. The national colors were used with the napkins, tablecloths and wherever else was appropriate.

Extra security was hired for the important occasion and two men were stationed in the kitchen, watching everything and everybody.

Since the royal couple was staying at the White House and was going to a later event, the party was scheduled from five to seven o'clock at the embassy.

On the stroke of five, several guests arrived, dressed to the nines and anxious to meet the honored couple. By 5:30, everyone was there when the royal twosome showed up. Everyone was lined up to meet and greet them.

As the party progressed, a small musical group could barely be heard above the talking and laughter. The waiters were kept busy passing hors d'euvres and drinks. The honored couple seemed to be enjoying themselves and were mixing well with the crowd.

About 6:15, the wife of the ambassador came into the kitchen all aflutter, saying what a wonderful party it had turned out to be. She told Joe that he was doing a great job and everyone was having a marvelous time. She was concerned that they had run out of the pate de foie gras and wanted to know if more were available. In fact, she told Joe that a French diplomat remarked that it was the best pate' he had eaten since leaving Paris. He commented to the hostess that it couldn't be American. It certainly must have been imported from France.

Joe thought to himself that they were not serving pate'. It must have been something else the Frenchman had commented on. He told the ambassador's wife that he would look into it as she left to join the other guests.

Joe went into the pantry to check on the food supply. His search proved nothing. He asked the cooks if anyone had prepared any pate'. All responded negatively.

Joe asked one of the waiters to go into the dining room, remove the pate' platter and bring it into the kitchen. After a few minutes, the waiter returned with the empty plate. A small residue remained on the dish and spreader. Joe scooped up a smidgen with his finger and tasted it. There was no question that it was pate' de foie gras. He scraped another finger across the plate and smelled it. It was definitely liver.

Joe noticed that one of the South American waiters was busy replenishing a vegetable tray. In communicating with him, Joe found out that the waiter had made a spread out of some cans of liverwurst that he had found in the pantry. He pointed to the trash receptacle in which he had

The Royal Visit

discarded the empties. Joe reached down and pulled out a small used container that read "Cat Food, Beef and Liver Flavored". It was a well-known American brand with a prominently displayed picture of a kitten.

He started to confront the South American waiter about what he had done. Who authorized him to make anything? Why did he do it? Didn't he know it was cat food? Even if he couldn't read English, didn't he see the picture of the cat on the can?

If this got out, especially to the media, it could become an international incident. After all this was at a party in a foreign embassy and honoring popular members of the royal family. What an embrassment.

Joe then thought to himself. What could he do. First, cool it. Think about it. Don't over react. Get control of yourself. He remembered his Navy training. In a crisis, remain calm. Think logically about the situation before taking any action or doing anything foolish.

He continued to worry over it, but thinking that if no one finds out about it, no one will know. Why tell anybody, including the cooks and waiters? After all, it wasn't poison. Cats eat it all the time and seem to thrive on it. Maybe it will be all right for humans, too.

Joe fished out all the cans and ran water over them to remove the paper labels which he

Funny Bone

promptly flushed down the toilet. He dropped the twelve empty tins into a plastic bag and personally took it out to the dumpster. He was trusting no one with the evidence.

After he regained his composure and was in full control of himself, Joe smiled as he thought of the Frenchman who remarked that it was the best pate this side of Paris.

If he only knew.

Duke's Day

Duke was having his 65th birthday and his wife Stella was giving him a party on the following Saturday night. Her invitation was very specific – no presents.

She had planned a rather nice affair and had requested that the men wear a coat and tie. It wasn't a formal event, but the women were expected to dress accordingly. Certainly, this was a special occasion and Stella wanted to do it with pizzazz. I was looking forward to it. They had always been marvelous hosts and gave great parties.

In the world of senior citizens, becoming sixty-five is a landmark year. That is the time that one goes on Medicare and becomes eligible to receive Social Security benefits. Also, many people retire from their lifetime jobs and start getting their benefits from private pensions. So, it's an achievement and a wonderful time for a celebration.

Both Duke and Stella were our special friends. I couldn't go to his birthday party and not take a present, even a fun type one. Even though his wife ruled out bringing anything, I decided to buy him an inexpensive, silly gift. I didn't have anything in mind so I went to the Dollar Tree, a store that sells everything for one dollar. You have never seen so many items. They carry everything from toys, kitchen gadgets, clothing to packaged foods, and all for the same low price.

It was fascinating just looking at everything. I couldn't believe that some of the items only cost a dollar. Many were well known advertised national brands. How could they sell so cheap? It was intriguing.

The first thing I picked up was a cut out paper doll book. The model was a shapely young girl in a brief bathing suit. Throughout the book, there were various dresses and outfits to be used for dressing the doll. I thought that this might be appropriate since Duke and Stella had no daughters, only sons. Then, I thought maybe not. Anyway, it was to be a joke.

I looked in the toy section and saw several playthings that would be suitable and funny before moving over to the birthday novelties on display. There, I found exactly what I was looking for. It was a round white candle over 2 inches high and over four inches across, decorated exactly like a regular birthday cake. There were colored flowers around the edges with a big 'Happy Birthday" written in the center. Everything was wax. It sat on a white paper doily that looked like lace. It also came with a few regular small colored candles that were coordinated with the fancy trimmings. It was the perfect birthday gift and the price was right. Only one dollar.

I was so impressed with it that I bought all the three that were on display. I wanted a total of five for future use so I asked the sales clerk if there were more available. She went into the back room to check and returned to report that I was buying the last three of them. She did not know if any were on order, but I should telephone her or come by the store again in about ten days.

The night of the party, my wife and I lit three of

the small candles, one for the present, one for the past and one for the future. We walked into the party with the lighted cake, singing "Happy Birthday". Everyone saw what we were doing and joined in. It was a big hit.

Duke worked his way through the crowd and came over to us. He took the "cake" and blew out the candles.

Grinning, he exclaimed, "This is really great. Thank you so much."

Stella joined us, "I should have known that you two would do something special like this. It's wonderful."

With Duke and Stella at my side, our friend Mitzi came over, examined the cake and complimented me on it.

"Where in the world did you get that?", pointing to the candle. "It's the cleverest thing I've seen."

There I was, talking to our hosts. I was reluctant to say that I had bought it at the Dollar Tree. Duke and Stella would have enjoyed hearing it, but I was determined that I was not going to tell.

I replied, "At the mall."

"Which store?"

I responded that it was a new store and I did not remember its name.

Mitzi continued to quiz me. "Was it in the mall or one of those stores outside?"

I was caught off guard with my little white lie

and responded, "Outside."

"What other store was it near?"

I wondered when this inquisition was going to end. I was not about to tell her that I bought it at the Dollar Tree. Duke was still standing next to me, listening to the whole conversation. I stood my ground.

"The drugstore."

"Which side of the drugstore? Up toward the bookstore or down toward that new shoestore?"

I was getting a bit exasperated and was thinking of a store that would sell party accessories. Each answer just fueled another question.

I couldn't think of anything. My mind went blank.

"I don't remember." I was tired of lying and thought that I had better move on, still not wanting to divulge my secret.

"Please excuse me. I need something to drink."

I walked away from them and mixed in with the others in the crowd as I gave a sigh of relief.

Guests told me how cute the wax cake was and wanted to know where it came from. They wanted to get one, too. When I told them it was bought at The Dollar Tree, Mitzi overheard my remark.

She moved closer and said, "Now I know why you were acting so vague. I thought something was wrong the way you acted. At The Dollar Tree store. That's where all items sell for a dollar.

Right?"

I shook my head and said, "You finally got the picture."

Smiling, she remarked, "I apologize for giving you the third degree, but I think it's the cleverest thing I've ever seen. I'm going over to the store in the morning and get me a couple of them."

"Your apology is accepted. No need to go tomorrow because I bought the last three that they had in the store. And there were no more in the warehouse. Sorry."

Mitzi shook her head and remarked, "You devil, you."

High School Reunion

A 50th reunion of my high school class in Oxford, North Carolina was being planned for the following spring. I was looking forward to it. It had been many years since I had seen most of my fellow classmates, although a few of us had kept in touch over the years. Those were the ones who had continued to live in our hometown.

After several weeks of organizing the affair,

invitations were sent out to those who could be located. Then, the telephone kept ringing to inquire if I was planning to go. All of my former buddies were encouraging me to join them for the festivities.

Since my wife grew up in another part of the state, she would not know very many people there, but she wanted me to see my long ago friends. Also, she knew that her own high school reunion would take place in another two years, and it would be easier to get me to go with her if she went to mine. She had mixed feelings about going, but decided it was the best thing to do.

The reunion was a lot of fun and a big success. After returning home, there were many people and wonderful stories to be remembered. One attendee told us that she recalled the saying about one going back to one's high school reunion: "If you can't go back looking thin, then go back looking rich." From the response from the crowd, I think a lot of people agreed with her.

Dorothea Smithers, an average looking girl in high school appeared as the glamour girl of the party. She was decked out in a slinky tight fitting white satin jumpsuit and caused a minor sensation. Most of the women thought she looked a bit flashy, but all of the men drooled over her. No one could believe she had changed into such an alluring and dazzling human being.

High School Reunion

And then, our youthful mathematics teacher admitted to having had a facelift during the past year. She was at least 75 years old and looked as young, if not younger, than most of her ex-students.

Most of the guys were somewhat caught off guard when they saw Fred Gearhiser, the former handsome jock who was the delight of every girl in the class. Not only had he lost all of his curly black hair, he also sported the largest beer gut at the gathering. His stomach was so huge you couldn't see his belt.

He was very personable and well liked by all, but we boys had always been a little jealous. It was a known fact that every girl had a crush on him at one time or another. Those of us who weren't bald or too fat were remembering and smiling.

The popular and former class clown, Louise Jeffreys, regaled everyone when she told about some of her experiences. After the death of her husband, she had gone into a complete decline for several months before turning her life around. She stopped feeling sorry for herself and decided to take a Caribbean cruise with a lifetime friend who also was a widow. When she got home from her trip, she returned to her former busy life, volunteering at her church, delivering meals to shut-ins and rejoining her weekly card club. She definitely got her life back together. Since she was alone, she went to movies in the afternoon rather than at night. She felt much safer driving to and from the theater while it was still daylight.

Louise told us that on one occasion, she went to a matinee at the theater and sat in an empty seat on the aisle next to an older man. Since it was dark, she couldn't see very well so couldn't determine if she knew him or not. After about a half-hour, the man reached over and pinched her.

Someone asked, "What did you do, Louise?"

She responded, "Well, I just pinched him back and moved my seat."

Everyone laughed.

After the banquet was over, everyone was called upon to stand up and tell about himself or herself. You could talk as long as you wanted to about yourself and your children, but were limited to two and a half minutes regarding your grandchildren.

One of our former classmates, Gwen Atkins, was a petite redhead when in high school. After fifty years, she had turned into a mammoth creature. She looked gigantic in her lime green tent-like dress with her platinum blonde hair. I couldn't believe it was Gwen. She proudly informed us that she had three sons and all three were Presbyterian ministers. It seemed unbelievable.

Silly prizes were given to the person who had the most children, and grandchildren, the youngest

High School Reunion

looking of the returning students and the one who had traveled the farthest to come to the reunion.

The winner of the travel award was Earle Crews who had lived in Europe for many years. . As he passed by our table to receive his prize, someone sniped, "Look at his hair. You can tell it's dyed."

Someone else at our table retorted, "Would you believe that's not his hair. It's a wig. See how thick it is? People our age don't have hair like that."

The most satisfying part of the evening occurred when door prizes were given, the last thing on the program. The most unpopular and disliked person in our class was a sarcastic and mean spirited girl named Pearl Jackson. She was always putting everyone down with her caustic remarks, which constantly irked me, and I always wondered why she was like that. Sometimes I really felt sorry for her. She had no friends and no one liked her. I could never figure her out.

There she was, winning a door prize. Pearl walked up to the front as if she were receiving an academy award. She did not know that the back of her dress had been caught up in her pantyhose, showing her backside from the waist down. Nobody missed seeing the over-exposed posterior. The crowd went wild. Everyone was shouting, whistling and laughing. When Pearl found out what had happened, she rushed out of the room. It couldn't have happened to a more deserving person.

I remarked that the reunion had really been fun and an eye opener. It was wonderful being with all of my former classmates and to see how much they had changed over the years. I wouldn't have missed it for anything.

Thinking about her own to be held in two years, my wife finally muttered, "I can't wait for mine."

Twirling Tassels

Participating in the United States Army Reserve program meant going to summer camp for training for two weeks every year with one's own military unit. This was in addition to the four-hour weekly drill time at the local armory. Summer camp was called "annual training". It was very important to attend, otherwise, our organization would not be able to perform at its best. It was at the annual summer training that we would be graded on our performance as if we were fulltime soldiers. Efficiency reports were a big factor in determining promotions, not only in grade and rank, but also in more responsible positions within the military structure.

One summer, our Reserve group was ordered to Ft. Knox, Kentucky for two weeks. Instead of taking the troop train from my hometown, I decided to leave a few days earlier and drive my car so that I could stop and visit some friends along the way.

Having my car at camp gave me a great deal of freedom during my time on duty as well as at night and during the weekend. Our tour of duty began on the weekend and ended two weeks later. It was too far to drive home during the middle weekend so it was nice having my own transportation available.

One of my Army buddies was a dentist named Ned Barr. He was serious minded and somewhat of an intellectual. We hit it off when we had met a few years earlier. I respected him and thought he had a great sense of humor. Besides that, he always laughed at my jokes.

One evening, we decided to drive into Louisville for dinner at a restaurant that had been highly recommended to us. It was nice getting away from the hectic military life at Ft, Knox for a few hours and back into the civilian world.

Twirling Tassels

After we had finished our meal, we drove around the downtown area for a quick tour of the city. We saw the watermark of the great flood on the wall of the famous Brown's Hotel, West Main Street with its interesting 19th century cast iron architecture, the riverfront and other popular Louisville landmarks.

After our sightseeing jaunt, we crossed over the Ohio River bridge to the town of Jeffersonville, Indiana. The whole idea was just a lark. It was too tempting to both of us not to cross the river and go into another state. Since we had no agenda, there were no time constraints. We made a quick U-turn after the crossing that took us back to Kentucky.

As we headed back to Ft. Knox, we passed an establishment that advertised "live entertainment" with exotic girl dancers. The place looked a bit garish with its flashing and bubbling neon signs, but we both looked at one another and said, "Why not?"

When we walked into the building, we were met by a heavily made-up older blonde in a long black dress with shiny silver flecks. It was obvious that she picked that particular outfit since it was so low cut at the neck it showed off her dominant features. I'm sure she needed a large D-size bra, whether or not she was wearing one. I couldn't help but wonder why she didn't fall out.

"Good evening, sugars," she smiled. "Do you prefer a table or the bar?"

"A table will be fine," Ned responded.

After she had seated us, she remarked, "The show will start in about ten minutes. Can I get you something to drink?"

We each ordered a beer and looked around the dark place. There was a stage partially filled with a piano, a set of drums and other band instruments in front of a dark blue curtain. A horseshoe bar surrounded the stage with approximately twenty seats.

"Maybe we should have chosen the bar," I remarked.

Ned agreed. "It's definitely a front row seat. I always thought the bar was where they made the drinks."

"Me, too. Let's move our seat."

When the bosomy hostess had finished with two other customers, I caught her eye and motioned her over. I explained that this was our first visit and we didn't understand the difference between the table and the bar seating.

"We would like to move to the bar."

"Sure, cutie, that's no problem." she pointed to two bar seats.

"Since this your first time, take those two, the best seats in the house."

She explained that we could not take our beers

Twirling Tassels

with us when we moved. It was a state law. Only employees of the establishment were allowed to move them.

She seated us at the top curve in the horseshoe, looking directly at the band. We both agreed that she was right. These were the best seats in the house.

After several minutes, the room was filled to capacity including all twenty bar seats. The band members came on the stage and tested their instruments. After they had finished, the bright stage lights came on, then a loud drum roll. Out bounced the master of ceremonies, a short man in a glittering tuxedo with the slickest black hair I'd ever seen.

He welcomed everyone and cracked a few off-color jokes, half of which I had heard before. He assured everyone that we were in for a real treat. Tonight was going to be a special show and we were lucky to be there to enjoy it.

Then, another drum roll and the introduction of a superstar who had come to Louisville after a sensational run at an unfamiliar Miami Beach nightclub.

From behind the dark curtain, a gigantic blonde appeared, dressed as a college May Queen, a long fluffy light blue dress, long white gloves and the biggest matching picture hat imaginable. With the band playing, she pranced around the stage a few times before removing her hat, which she caressed tenderly.

After exhausting this maneuver, she coyly removed one of her long gloves and whirled it around and around, in front and on both sides. She finally tossed it behind the dark blue backdrop curtain. She did the same routine with the other one. All the time, she cavorted to the drummer's beat, bumping, grinding and wiggling and never missing a beat. She was over six feet tall and nearly broke me up when she lifted both arms and touched the ceiling with her hands. She looked as if she were actually holding up the roof.

A few more items of clothing were removed before she left the stage in a bikini outfit. As she departed, she gave a final bump. Even though she was big, she had a beautiful, well-proportioned body. After the final bump, the audience went wild.

Ned and I joined in the applause. I hollered and whistled with the others. Ned just smiled and shook his head.

The master of ceremonies returned to the microphone with his same corny jokes, introducing the next act, a singer who had some Hollywood credentials. It sounded as if she was a headliner. When she walked out on the stage, Ned and I were surprised to see the same bosomy hostess that had greeted us when we came in and who had moved

Twirling Tassels

our beers to the bar.

She sang a couple of oldies, one slow, the other upbeat. She had a fairly good voice but was drowned out frequently by the over zealous band. She was definitely playing to the audience of boisterous men, shaking her shoulders and blowing kisses to her individual admirers. It was obvious then that she was not wearing a bra.

She was well received and came back for an encore. She sang a serious religious song which she dedicated to someone in the audience. I thought it to be totally inappropriate for the occasion.

After she took her final bow, the master of ceremonies appeared and announced the next performer – the Tiger Girl.

Out comes a very thin girl dressed in a brief yellow and black striped tiger costume. A long tail was attached to her tight shorts, her hands were in gloves that were supposed to look like tiger paws, her headgear looked like a band with tiger ears, and each breast had a yellow and black hanging tassel.

Her talent was twirling the tassels. With no help from her paws, she began twirling both in the same direction. Then only the right one by itself. Next, the left one by itself. The big finale was twirling both in the same direction before changing to each one in the opposite direction – one going

Funny Bone

clockwise, the other counter clockwise.

I nudged Ned, "What do you think of that?"

In all seriousness, Ned replied, "she has a malocclusion."

"A malocclusion. What's that?"

He responded, "She has an over-bite."

I thought, "After all, he is a dentist." I didn't even notice her mouth. Too interested in those twirling tassels.

Even today when people tell me that they have an over-bite, my mind wanders. I think back about that Louisville tiger.

And smile.

Handsome Harry

Back in the 1970's, I made a deal with a real estate developer of a project containing a few hundred moderately priced bungalows. It was my job to hold an open house every Sunday afternoon for interested purchasers. A local store had provided the furniture and decorations in the model home with the understanding that they would be provided with the names of all future

Funny Bone

buyers of the houses. It cost the developer nothing to have a nicely furnished model. It also made the property more appealing from a sales standpoint.

My agreement was that every house sold through the open for inspection undertaking would entitle me to a sales commission from the developer. In addition, I would be in a very favorable position to get a sales listing of the purchaser's present home. It was a win-win situation for me to spend a few hours on a Sunday afternoon.

The houses were advertised in the newspaper each Sunday as being for sale and open for viewing that afternoon. I put 'OPEN' signs in prominent places on the property when I arrived each week. My automobile was parked in the street directly in front with a portable sign on the car roof, including an arrow pointing to the house. It was almost too much, but it drew people in.

The attractive furnishings were carefully selected throughout to give a feeling of openness and spaciousness to each room. The curtains, draperies and bed coverings were color coordinated with the décor of the entire house.

In the smallest bedroom, the folding closet doors were faced with floor to ceiling mirrors. It made the room look twice its size. I thought that was a clever idea. The interior decorator did a great job. The house showed off very well.

In the living room, several easels held the different architectural floor plans and exteriors of the properties including color charts and sample floor tiles. Attractive printed brochures with color photographs, floor plans and other important information about the houses were placed on a table for distribution. The sales program was well planned and organized. It made my job a lot easier.

On one occasion, a couple in their forties came in to tour the model. They were extremely interested in all aspects of the property, checking the various floor plans as well as studying the brochures for more information on the houses. They asked many questions before telling me that they were immensely interested in buying and that they would contact me later. They examined everything inside and out, even looking underneath the house. They walked around the entire yard before leaving

I expected to hear from them in the very near future.

The following week, I called them to see how things were progressing. I didn't want to appear over anxious, but I didn't want that sale to slip away. I even suggested that we put a "hold" on the specific house that they wanted to buy. I explained that it would cost them nothing and that we would not sell to anyone else for a 30-day period. They turned my suggestion down but said that they were still very interested in the house and would call me within the week.

They did call to tell me that they had decided to purchase the house. First, they had to sell their present home, or at least secure a sales contract on it. The purchase of the new house was dependent on the sale of their present home within 90 days.

Before listing it with me, they wanted to contact a few acquaintances that had shown some interest in it. They were not sure any of the group would be interested in buying but thought that they would give them an opportunity to say yes or no. Knowledge that their house was definitely for sale should create some interest in it. They wanted to hold everything in limbo for at least ten days. That much time should be more than sufficient to find out if anyone was seriously considering purchasing it.

Two weeks later, the couple telephoned and invited me to meet them at their home for an inspection. They wanted to find out what price they should ask for it. They had some ideas of their own but were eager to hear my thoughts on it.

We met one afternoon after they returned from work. After looking the house over carefully, I sat with them in the dining room with various documents spread across the table. There was a plat of the lot, a copy of their title insurance policy

Handsome Harry

as well as paid invoices on improvements made during the past several years. I also had a list of similar houses that had been sold during the past year in the general neighborhood.

They were aware of most of the properties and compared them to their house. Every reason was given to show how much more their house was worth compared to the one under discussion. This one was not centrally air-conditioned, that one did not have a fenced yard, another had been rented and left in horrible condition. The justifications went on and on.

After much discussion back and forth, I told them what I thought the house would bring on the current real estate market. They wanted a little more for it, so we finally agreed to add an additional five percent to the suggested price. They understood that it was higher than I had recommended, but it gave them some room to negotiate.

While I was writing up the formal agreement, the wife turned to her husband, nodded and said, "He sure looks like Harry, doesn't he?"

They were looking at me and talking about me. I had no idea who Harry was.

Her husband responded, "He sure does. When I first saw him at the model, I thought he sure looks like Harry."

They were both staring at me. I did not know

what to say, but I felt like I should say something.

So, I remarked, "Well, Harry must really be a handsome guy."

I smiled at myself and thought how clever I was with my remark.

In unison, they both replied, "No, Harry isn't handsome at all,"

Both were shaking their head, "No, not at all."

I don't think they realized how that sounded to me – "You look like Harry. But, Harry isn't handsome at all."

Me and my big mouth.

So much for cleverness.

Versailles Excursion

Our daughter Mary had finished her four years of college and decided to move to Paris. She was an art major but had a minor in French and felt that the art world beckoned from the Left Bank. Being able to communicate in the language was no drawback. Besides, she had a girl friend who had moved there and loved it.

She was told that the French were extremely interested in hiring American or British young

Funny Bone

people to look after their children. It was a great opportunity for the young ones to learn English at such an early age. There were many job openings from part-time work for a few days per week to full time live-in positions. The demand for both was high, the supply low.

Mary didn't take much coaxing to go. She had made up her mind early on that she would give it a try. It was now or never. Off she went to France with great plans and great expectations, but not with great finances.

After arriving there and visiting her college friend for a few days, she accepted a job as a live-in *au pair* for a couple with two small children. Both parents worked for the French airline, Air France. He as an accountant, she as a flight attendant. They also had a full time maid so the nanny job was not as demanding as it could have been. In addition to her duties, Mary was able to attend a French language class at the Alliance Francaise. It was a perfect setup.

After several months, my wife and I made plans to visit her. We had been to Paris previously and had such wonderful memories of doing all the things tourists do. It was a wonderful city. Of course, there were many things we did not do before and looked forward to new experiences as well as seeing our daughter.

We made reservations at a pleasant small hotel

Versailles Excursion

in the Montparnasse section of Paris near where she lived. We thought the room was adequate and cozy, but a bit small by American standards. We were on the fourth floor so the elevator was a needed luxury. In France, the first floor is what is known in America as the second floor. What we call the first floor is actually the ground floor all through Europe. So, the first floor is up one flight of stairs from the ground floor. The second floor, two flights up, and so on. In Paris, being on the fourth floor was too many steps for us to climb at our age.

When our daughter came to our hotel room, she could not believe that the room was so large and spacious. We were somewhat amused with her remark, but understood what she meant. She had been living in France for several months and had forgotten how big everything is in America, including hotel and motel rooms.

My wife and I decided to sign up with a travel agency for a half-day excursion to Versailles. When Mary heard the price and converted it to American money, she said it was too much to pay. We should go on our own at a fraction of the cost. She had taken the train for about two dollars round trip and had visited the palace with some friends. We told her that it was best for us to take the commercial excursion since we did not know our way around and knew only a few phrases in

French. Besides, how would we know how to get to the chateau when we got off the train. She informed us that the palace could be seen from the station, and all we had to do was walk straight down the street to it. It wasn't a large town or a long walk from the station.

She did not tell us that the street was lined with gift shops, bookstores, restaurants and other kinds of retail shops. It was set up for tourists to stop and spend their francs.

My wife and I talked about it during the day and finally decided to go by ourselves and forget about the guided tour. All we wanted to do was to see the palace anyway. We would take the train down and get a ticket for a tour with an English speaking guide to see the building and gardens. Mary thought we had made the right decision.

The Montparnasse train station was three blocks from our hotel and adjoining the tallest building in Paris. Luckily for us, the skyscraper was a landmark. When we did not know where we were, we could look up and identify which way to go. In fact, when we were at the top of the Eiffel Tower with its spectacular view, we could clearly see the neighborhood in which we were staying. I think the high-rise office building was the tallest in Paris at that time and not very well liked by the French people.

When traveling in foreign countries, I dress in

Versailles Excursion

dark, conservative casual clothes. Black or gray slacks, a maroon or charcoal sweater and either a blazer or windbreaker is the style for the day. No flashy or bright colors, no college sweatshirts, no logos. Nothing to bring any attention. I want to meld into the crowd.

On several occasions while overseas in non-speaking English countries, people who wanted some directions have come up and asked, "Excuse me, but do you speak English?"

I always replied yes that I did speak English, was an American and it was my native tongue.

Somewhat shocked, many responded that I looked like a local, not at all like an American. Maybe it was the low key demeanor of those dark clothes.

With that on my mind, I wanted to try an experiment: pass myself off as a Frenchman. My wife could not understand why I wanted to do such a silly thing. She thought the idea was crazy. What was the point of it? I was an American tourist and there was nothing wrong with that.

I explained about the number of people who had come up to me in the past, thinking I was a native. I had never tried to convince anyone that I was anything but what I was. This would be a game, just to see if I could pass as a Frenchman. All for fun and amusement and to see if it would be a success.

Funny Bone

    Without my wife's usual support, I set the scene. With a black beret covering my head and a folded French newspaper under my arm, I thought I looked like a native Parisan. Of course, the newspaper was a prop, definitely not for reading. My wife was not to speak to me except to say *"Oui"* or *"No"*. If she spoke any English, then the people would know we were not French. This was only when we were encountering the natives. Out of hearing range, speaking normally was fine.

    I didn't plan to go into my act until we arrived at Versailles. When we boarded the train in Paris, I didn't wear my beret or tuck the newspaper under my arm, just traveled as the all American boy.

    The train itself was very different from those in the United States. The railroad car was divided into two levels. You entered in the center on the side and either stepped up to the left on one side or stepped down to the right on the other side. In each of the areas, the seats faced the front and were set by the windows on either side with an aisle between them. We rode in the down area going, and the up area returning.

    The train was not crowded with only a few people in each of the sections. A young man across the aisle heard us talking and asked if he could practice his English with us. He had taken courses in school for the past three years and had learned a great deal. His French accent was very

Versailles Excursion

noticeable but it was difficult to understand everything he said.

He did very well in spite of it and I gave him high marks for trying. `In reflection, he succeeded in communicating which is more than we could do in his language.

We explained some American slang expressions which he had learned from watching television programs. When we left at our destination, he thanked us and said good-by. I almost flipped when he added, "Have a nice day." It was then when I realized he had picked up a lot from TV.

As soon as we stepped off the train, I became Monsieur Francais

As we left the station, we saw the palace in front of us, straight down the street. I adjusted my beret, tucked the newspaper under my arm and started toward the main tourist attraction.

There were people from the station walking in front and behind us, speaking English, French and other languages. Some went into the shops, some kept on toward the chateau.

After a few minutes down the street, a Frenchman with a menu in his hand was inviting the tourists to come into his restaurant. He was speaking French. When he saw us, he greeted us with beautiful English, "We have an English menu and welcome all people from England."

Didn't he see I was French. What about my

beret and my French newspaper? Why was he speaking English to us?

I was taken by surprise with him giving his sales pitch. Not to be outdone, I smiled and greeted him with a vigorous *"Bon Jour"*.

"Bon Jour to you, too," he responded in English. "We think it's wonderful when you Brits speak French to us."

As we walked on a bit, my wife turned to me and asked, "Since you're a Brit, is it all right for me to speak English now?"

The Square Piano

My Uncle Walter had always had an old square rosewood piano in his parlor. He never played it so it had deteriorated to the point that no one could pick out a song on it. It was never tuned and the white keys had turned yellow with age. The wooden cabinet had been dusted every now and then, but it had never been treated or waxed. Since his wife had gone to her reward many years before, Uncle Walter just did not care about the piano. It originally belonged to Aunt Hettie's family, the Mills. Since they had no children, Uncle Walter inherited everything from her, the house, her jewelry, and all furnishings, including the piano. Some the Mills family thought that Uncle Walter should have shared some of their family belongings with them, particularly since Aunt Hettie had no heirs of her own.

Uncle Walter thought that if Aunt Hettie wanted her own family to have anything, she would have told him about it or left specific bequeaths in her will. He was convinced that she left him everything so he could do what he wanted to do.

The local historical group had approached him about donating the unusual antique piano to the museum in memory of Aunt Hettie. He told them he would think about it, but never made a decision during his lifetime. I think he was irritated with the members who constantly hounded him about it. One time I had mentioned how nice it would be if he gave it to the museum, only to be told to mind my own business.

"Who put you up to this?" he asked.

"Put me up to what?" I responded.

"I know some of those busybodies from the museum got you to try and get me to give them the piano."

I was a little taken back by his quick and indignant remark.

The Square Piano

"No one put me up to anything. And don't be so uptight about it. If you're not going to fix it up and have it tuned, then it should go to the museum. At least they appreciate the piano which is more than you do."

Apologetically, he said, "If you only knew what I've been through with those people. They drive me crazy. Every time I see one of those members, they always harass me about giving them the piano. They never let up."

I did not say anything and resolved that I would never again mention the museum and the piano in the same sentence. It was a sore subject and it would upset him too much.

When I was young and visited Uncle Walter and Aunt Hettie, I was fascinated with the piano. Even then, it was out of tune, but it was fun to pick out a song with one finger. The size and its odd shape made the piano interesting and attractive. I had never seen one like it.

Through the years, I warmly remembered it. One summer, I was sent to Kentucky for two weeks with my Army Reserve unit. During the weekend, I went to Bardstown where I toured Federal Hill, a plantation house that later became known as "My Old Kentucky Home". Stephen Foster had stayed with his cousin who lived there and it was presumed that Foster had been inspired to compose his famous song during the visit.

Funny Bone

When I walked into the music room, the guide pointed to a square piano. I thought of Uncle Walter and Aunt Hettie since the piano was exactly like theirs except for the keys. The ones in Kentucky were mother of pearl, Uncle Walter's were ivory. The same firm must have made them since they were identical in shape and size and both cabinets were made of rosewood. However, there was no comparison in the condition of the two. Perfect versus neglected.

After returning home, I went by to see Uncle Walter. I told him about the piano in Kentucky and asked about the early history of his. He didn't know anything about it, except that it came from the Mills home.

My mind went searching. Where and when did they get it? Why did they buy it? Who in the family played it? I thought maybe we were on to something, but Uncle Walter knew absolutely nothing about it and knew of no one in Aunt Hettie's family he could ask. All of her generation had died. Only the grandchildren and great grandchildren were around and he was assured that they weren't interested in it and wouldn't know anything about it.

I told him that I always had been attracted to the piano and had thought through the years that it was exceptional. Perhaps it was unique and worth a great deal of money.

The Square Piano

He sensed my enthusiasm and said if I wanted to look into it with the idea of selling it to go ahead. He wasn't unhappy about it since he admitted it was not his favorite possession.

I agreed to do a little investigating to find out anything that could shed some light on it.

For several weeks, I made inquiries concerning square pianos, visiting museums, stores, antique outlets and the public library. I found out that this type of piano was not uncommon. The one in Kentucky was made by the Ambler company. They were very popular in the early part of the 19th century and many were still around and in good condition.

I went by to tell Uncle Walter that it was not worth as much as I thought. If it had a special or noteworthy history, such as Stephen Foster composing one of his songs on it, the value would be high.

Uncle Walter informed me, "If you plan to tell people that 'Swanee River' or some other famous song was composed on it, I couldn't do it. It's not true."

I retorted, "How do you know that? It could have been."

He looked me straight in the eye, "Son, I couldn't do it, but there's nothing to stop you from doing it."

I was surprised at his remark, thought a minute,

then asked, "Which song would you prefer, 'Swanee River' or 'Camptown Races'?"

Without batting an eye, he answered, "How about 'Jail Time is Hard Time'?"

"I don't believe I've ever heard of it. Did Stephen Foster write it?"

Smiling, he replied, "No, Stephen Foster didn't write it. It will be written by you if you sell that piano under false pretenses."

We both chuckled.

The piano was never offered for sale. He decided not to push it, but if someone came and wanted to buy it, he would listen to all offers.

A few years later, Uncle Walter passed away and left the antique square piano to the local historical museum at his death.

He had a codicil added to his will with the notation that nothing important was ever composed on it.

He did get the last jab from his grave.

Doctor's Exchange

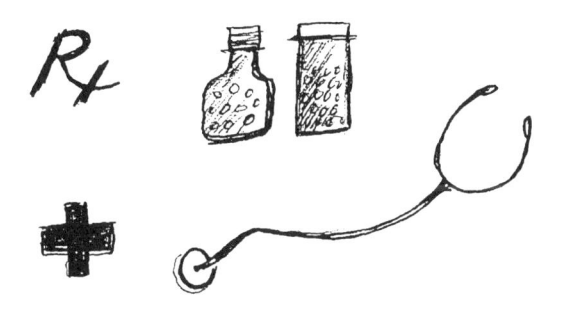

My friend Travis liked to have his cocktail every evening before dinner. Since he had retired from his 30-year stint at a local insurance agency, he just enjoyed a life that included a drink with his wife Maggie either on the patio in the summer or in the den by a crackling fire in the winter. Spring and fall were fun, too. It just depended on the weather, which it would be, inside or outside.
Either way, it was a pleasant time of the day for

both of them to enjoy each other's company for a brief time before heading for the kitchen to prepare the evening meal.

Travis and Maggie had decided to take a winter vacation in Florida after the first of the year. They had visited there a few times previously, but only stayed for a week to ten days since he was working and had to return to his job. This time, they planned to go for one month beginning the third week of January. They felt that it was an ideal time to seek a warmer climate until around the end of February. The weather at home was usually cold then, but began to improve after the first of March.

Ever since he retired, Travis religiously exercised every day. He had bought a walking machine and had turned part of his basement into a workout room. He walked three miles every day on the machine while watching his favorite television morning show. It was entertaining as well as good for his overall health. He felt fine and that he was in excellent physical shape for a man of his age.

He wanted to stay at a place in Florida that had an exercise room so that he could keep up his daily routine. While driving down, he also planned to walk his three miles each morning. If there were no fitness center there, he would walk outside. His habit had been formed and he had no intention of breaking it.

Several weeks before their ensuing trip, Travis had a fainting spell and just collapsed at home. Before it happened, he had been feeling fine and had not complained about feeling sick. Maggie was alarmed when he passed out so she called the rescue squad and sent him off to the emergency room at the hospital. He was checked out thoroughly by the medical staff on duty. They found nothing wrong with him and called his regular family physician. After his own doctor examined him, it was suggested that Travis remain in the hospital for a few extra days for additional testing and monitoring. Something might turn up which could shed some light on what caused him to faint.

When I heard the news, I went by to see him the day before he was discharged. His spirits were great and he said he was feeling fine. No one had found anything that caused him to pass out. His cardiogram, blood pressure, stress test and sugar level did not indicate any health problems. All of his vital signs were normal.

He wondered what caused his fainting but was pleased that everything was fine. Travis did tell me that the doctor questioned him about his exercise program and his eating and drinking habits. He was advised to watch his salt intake and his fat consumption. He was slightly overweight but only by a few pounds. His exercise program had helped in that category. He was also told to cut out all alcohol. No more cocktails, no more wine at dinner, and no more beer. Travis was somewhat shocked at this statement.

"You mean I can never drink again?" he asked the physician.

"Absolutely," responded the doctor. "Look what just happened to you. If you drink, it might kill you if you don't give it up completely. I cannot be more specific."

Travis nodded his head in agreement, but thought this was going to be devastating. He enjoyed having his drink every evening and had always understood that one or two drinks each day were good for you. It was relaxing and put a point on your appetite.

Travis kept thinking about his hospital visit and what the doctor had said about what he ate and drank. Since they never found out anything about what happened, he wondered why they were so concerned about his living habits. Everything had checked out normal. He was completely puzzled by it all but thought it best to do what the doctor said. He did not want to chance it.

Maggie had insisted that he follow the proper prescribed low salt and low fat diet. She thought it would be good for her, too. She had no health problems but was interested in losing a few pounds herself. Eliminating the cocktail time before dinner each evening posed no problem to her either.

They found a furnished one-bedroom beachfront condominium in Florida to rent for a month. It had been difficult to find a suitable place since most apartments required a minimum of a three months lease. They felt fortunate in finding what they wanted and where they wanted to be. It also had a health spa on the premises. Both were happy.

A few weeks later, the couple drove to Florida and remained there for a month.

When they returned home around the end of February, they telephoned and invited my wife and me over for dinner one evening. They were anxious to tell us about their trip. The weather had been wonderful the entire time they were there. They had a great time, but were happy to be back home again.

When we arrived at their home, we were warmly greeted and ushered into the den. Travis handed me a handful of photographs he had taken on their trip and wanted us to see.

"While you are drooling over the pictures, what can I get you to drink?" our host asked.

We responded with our order as we looked at the pictures. They were typical of Florida – the beautiful blue water, white sandy beaches and many, many palm trees. Both Travis and Maggie, one or the other, were in most of them. They were so beautiful and inviting, it made me want to visit there.

I noticed that Travis poured himself a vodka and tonic cocktail.

I said, "I thought the doctor told you to cut out alcohol completely."

He smiled, "He did, but I went to another doctor in Florida and he told me it was all right to drink if I didn't overdo it."

"Then, you changed doctors," I noted.

Lifting his glass, he toasted, "Yes, I changed. Here's to the doctors who know how to live!"

Lopez

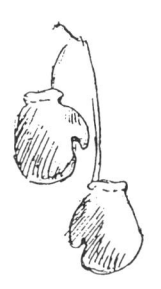

When I was nineteen years old, I was serving in the United States Army. My assignment was at a language school at the University of Wisconsin, studying Italian.

Even though we were in the middle of World War II, being in the Army course was what was known as soft duty. We had it easy compared to our fellow soldiers who were fighting on the European front and in the Pacific. At least, no one

Funny Bone

was shooting at us.

All of us were aware of our situation and felt very lucky and privileged to be in school. We knew that if we failed any of our courses or didn't tow the line, we would be transferred out to a regular military fighting unit. It gave us a great incentive to be interested in what we were doing, to study hard and stay out of trouble.

During wartime, we were always required to wear our uniform, both on duty and off. In fact, no one even had any civilian clothes. They were all bundled up and sent home on the first day of induction into the service.

Classes involving Italian vocabulary, grammar, history and geography were held throughout the day, taught by regular civilian professors at the school. Some were from the old country and could barely speak English. Of course, their Italian was superb, and they were good role models from the language standpoint. Later on when we worked with real Italian soldiers, it was easier for us to communicate with them because of our association with the genuine thing in school.

Since we were on active duty in the Army, military discipline was strongly enforced. We arose very early every day for reveille and later were marched in formation to our meals and classes. Regular inspections and military training were given constantly by active duty professional soldiers.

Even though we were quartered in a former fraternity house, it was more like a barracks. The entire building had been stripped of furnishings and decorations before being turned over to the government for military use. No carpeting, no window curtains, no pictures and no privacy. The rooms were like dormitories with metal wardrobes, footlockers and four double deck bunks, each shared by two soldiers. There were eight people in every room. It was not like being in college at all.

Our classes were scheduled, but we did have a choice for our physical training, either boxing class or ice-skating. Being from the South, I was not used to sub-zero weather or frozen lakes, so I decided to stay in the warm gymnasium and learn how to fight. I had been in a few schoolyard fisticuffs and thought it would be in my best interest to learn how to defend myself. There had been a bully in high school who picked on the younger and smaller students of which I was one. It would be just great to get the best of him when I got back home. Boxing class was definitely for me.

Our boxing coach was the epitome of a professional fighter. His physical appearance looked like he was built from the ground up. Powerful looking legs, a flat muscular stomach, narrow hips, full chest, and biceps that bulged as if they could lift 500 pounds. His face appeared to have received a million punches. Other than an obvious broken nose, he was a fine looking human specimen.

After a brief orientation on the sport of pugilism and the rules of the game, we were instructed to get a sparring partner. Pick out anyone. I looked around at the assembled group and checked out every one. While I was searching the crowd and sizing each one up, a tall guy asked me to be his partner. He was heavier and towered at least five or six inches above me. His arms were in proportion to his body and were much longer than mine. In my mind, I could visualize us boxing together. His long arms and my short ones. Thanks, but no thanks.

My eyes fell on a smaller, short young man. After all, at that time in my life, I was small and short, too. He looked about right size for me and appeared not to be such a great threat. His arms were about the same length as mine. I wandered over to him and asked him if he would be my sparring partner.

He sized me up for a minute or two before accepting my invitation. I think he thought about me as I had about him. Just the right size. We introduced ourselves. In the military, last names are always used unless it was a special friend or bosom buddy. His name was Lopez and he was from southern California.

Before joining the military, Lopez had finished high school and was going to college in his hometown. He had been a day student, worked part-time at a service station and lived with his parents who had emigrated from Mexico to San Diego.

Because of his family background, he was fluent in Spanish. We both thought it odd for him to be studying Italian, but he was selected to do so. He commented that this way was the Army way. No need to try and understand it.

Actually, at that time, there was a need for Italian interpreters since Italy was involved in the war. Spanish was not a high priority on the military requirement. I thought that at least Lopez speaks two languages so the Army must have had him categorized as a linguist. Why not? With his knowledge of Spanish, learning another romance language would surely come a lot easier for him than for me. The coach was explaining how to protect your body, especially your face. Blocking your opponent's punch was as important as your hitting him. We were told to keep a guard with one hand up in the vicinity of the face. Jab with the other hand. Since I was right handed it felt appropriate to strike with it while shielding with the left. Lopez and I practiced. He managed to hit me all over my body. He pounded me on my chest and slapped away at my stomach. He poked my forehead, both cheeks, jaw, mouth and nose. I never was able to lay a glove on him even though I tried. He was quick footed and maneuvered to avoid my swings. I bombed out in defending myself. How he managed to get past my guard was a mystery. Maybe I was too intent on slugging him, not thinking about anything else.

So went the first class.

A couple of days later, the next session was spent reviewing the previous lesson in protecting and guarding oneself. My partner and I started sparring again. It was a repeat of two days ago. I never was able to hit him while he was having a field day with me. I concentrated on my guard, hoping to minimize his contacts with me. It didn't work. I was relieved when the coach told us to stop.

"Lopez," I said exasperatingly, "I don't know what I'm doing wrong. I've never laid a glove on you."

"Don't worry, it will come. It takes time to get the feel of it," he responded.

"I sure hope so,"

Then the instructor talked about footwork. A boxer had to be able to move about quickly to avoid being hit. We practiced with an imaginary opponent, jabbing our hands in the air while bobbing with our feet. I rehearsed doing a right jab, then a quick left hook, jumping all the time. Our feet were moving to the front, back and from side to side. Everyone was bouncing around in rhythm. It was almost as if we were dancing. Maybe we were.

Then, we were told to get our partner and practice our footwork. I was looking forward to sparring with Lopez. Maybe my footwork would help me dodge his punches and give me an opportunity to hit him. I was sure hoping that my time had come.

We began jumping around each other, jabbing at one another. Again, I never was able to touch him while he was knocking me everywhere. His footwork and punching were fabulous. Every time I took a swat at him, I only hit air. He came back with at least two contacts with me.

I stopped him and asked, "Lopez, have you ever boxed before?"

He grinned, "A little bit."

"I thought so. You're great. I can't ever connect with you. Your guard is always up or you dodge my punch."

Still grinning, he replied, "Thank you. I think I should tell you something."

Looking like the cat that ate the canary, he continued, "You ought to know that before I came in the Army, I was a runner-up champion in the Southern California Golden Gloves matches."

Funny Bone

"Ouch."

I went over to the coach and asked if it was too late for me to switch to skating.

He tried to convince me to stay with the boxing class, but there were no more sparring partners available. Lopez was too experienced for me. Since everyone had found out about his Golden Gloves past, he could not get another partner himself so the coach made him his assistant.

Lopez and I became very good friends after our boxing debacle. I envied him for his fabulous fighting ability and admired him for his fierce determination, dry wit and old fashioned values.

After several weeks on frozen Lake Mendota, I became a fairly good ice skater.

Lopez was the anointed one in the boxing ring, no question about that. But he was not so great on the ice rink.

Happily and confidently, I could skate circles around him.

Cud'n Gillette

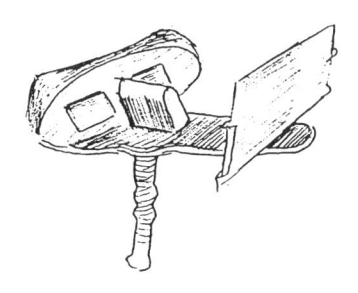

Gillette Thompson was a genteel lady of the Old South who was my grandmother's best friend. We all called her Cud'n Gillette, which was southern for Cousin Gillette. Even though she was not a relative, she did not want my family to call her Mrs. Thompson or Miss Gillette as others did. She preferred Cud'n.

In the southern way of life, it was standard to

refer to special friends as "Uncle", "Aunt" or "Cud'n" along with their given name. It was close and personal. My father and mother called her Gillette, but for us grandchildren, it was unquestionably Cud'n Gillette.

Other people who knew her well but were not special friends referred to her as "Miss" Gillette" rather than as the more formal "Mrs. Thompson." These were those acquaintances she dealt with in a day to day setting such as at the post office, the library, the grocery store, the service station and other business contacts.

Her husband had died right after World War I, so I knew him only through the many pictures and stories about him. His portrait in his military uniform hung majestically over the mantle in the living room of his former home. Colonel Thompson had been one of Teddy Roosevelt's soldiers and was a local hero of sorts. His wife was enormously proud of him.

Growing up in Oxford, North Carolina, I would visit Cud'n Gillette with my parents and was constantly fascinated with her conversations. She always had a funny story or two to tell, but I was continually charmed with her tales of her life when she was young. It was like living in another century with gas streetlights and horsedrawn buggies. It was wonderful to hear about her first ride in an early automobile. Equally interesting

Cud'n Gillette

was to learn of the advent of radio and what an impact it had on the world. Television came on the scene much, much later.

Cud'n Gillette's old photos were much better than reading a book. On the reverse of each, she had scrawled the names, dates and places shown on the front. It made them come to life and interesting. One of my favorites of her many possessions was an old stereoscope which showed three-dimensional pictures. The cards, which were dropped into a slot, comprised two images of the same subject side by side. When you looked through the eyepieces, the photos became life-like. It was captivating and pure magic, particularly to a young boy.

During our visits, she always brought out some wonderful treats. Cookies, cake, candy, custard pudding, and all homemade. Nothing was ever made from a prepared mix. Sometimes, she had ice cream which was hand turned in an old fashioned ice cream maker. It was a great thrill when she let me lick the dasher. All in all it was a great event to visit her.

As the years passed, my visits became fewer and farther apart. She moved into a retirement home in her late 80's. She had no children of her own, but her relatives convinced her that she should not live alone any longer. She had given up her driver's license and had sold her automobile. She felt her

Funny Bone

independence slipping away and finally agreed to move into a more leisurely lifestyle. Her attitude was positive, but it was sad for her to leave her home after so many years and so many happy memories.

Her health began to fail and she was experiencing some hearing loss.

I went to see her after she first moved into her new quarters. It was difficult to communicate since I had to talk very loud to make her understand. I suggested she get a hearing aid which would help her, only to be told that she already was wearing one. I didn't see it since her hair was over her ears, hiding it well.

"What a pity," I thought. "Not being able to hear even with a hearing aid.

Since she was approaching 90 years old, her doctor told her it was important for her to rest a lot and suggested that she take a nap every afternoon. She spryly told him, "I certainly will if I wake up in time."

Her doctor told me about it and we both had a good laugh. She'll take a nap if she wakes up in time. Cud'n Gillette was a true character.

One day, a friend came to see her while I was visiting there. The friend was telling about an incident that had occurred several years previously and mentioned the name Captain Jack Longstreet.

Cud'n Gillette listened to the lady and remarked,

"Oh, yes. I remember when Uncle Jack did that."

I asked, "You called Captain Longstreet 'Uncle Jack'. Was he your uncle?"

"Of course, he was my uncle. He was my father's brother."

"Oh," I said. "I didn't remember that you were a Longstreet, Cud'n Gillette."

She drew herself up, looked at me straight in the eye and sternly declared, "Not were a Longstreet, Sweetie. Am."

"What?"

"I am not 'were' a Longstreet," she avowed, emphasizing the were. Drawing herself up, she continued, "I have always been and am now a Longstreet."

I could only nod my head in agreement. I knew that her maiden name was Longstreet, but I always thought of her by her married name of Thompson. She was very proud to be a Longstreet. There was no question about that.

After that episode, she reminded me of it from time to time. Deep down, I know that she thought the Longstreet family was just a bit better than the Thompsons. Cud'n Gillette always got the best of me.

I went by for an unannounced visit when she celebrated her 92nd birthday. When I walked into her room, I shouted at the top of my voice, "Happy 92nd birthday!"

Funny Bone

She frowned, "Don't holler so loud. Modulate your voice. You sound like you're waking up the dead."

I asked quietly, "Can you understand me if I talk like this?"

"Of course I can. I have a new battery in my hearing aid. The old one was over three years old and just went out."

Why hadn't I thought about that before? That battery had been dead for two years. I had been hollering and screaming at her during all those visits, and because of one little battery.

I really felt stupid.

The Ultimate Put-down

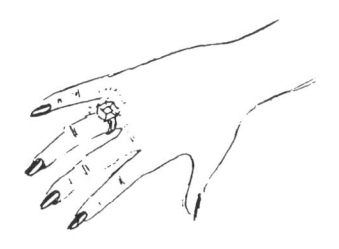

Dottie was a beauty, no question about it. She was tall, thin and blonde, and admitted to being 57 years old. According to her friends, she would never see 65 again. They knew that she qualified for Social Security and Medicare. Dottie never revealed that she was entitled to either one of them. She could be charming, particularly when she was in the company of men. She was a widow and missed her husband terribly. Dan had been killed in a small airplane crash a few years previously. Dottie went through a proper period of mourning and gradually moved back into the social scene. She adored going to parties and felt that if you want to be invited by others, you had to entertain. Pay back those who had entertained you. She did not want to be left out of any social gathering in her circle of friends so she entertained with a vengeance. She knew that everyone would include her on their list since all would be obligated to her. She saw to that.

Dottie was definitely a man's woman. She liked men. Women bored her. She even dressed for men. I never saw her with a long dress that did not have a slit up the skirt so she could show off her long, shapely legs. After years of trying to tease and tantalize men, she became an expert. She was no amateur. She knew how to get the attention she wanted.

Her actions angered women. Men thought she was terrific, lapping up all the attention and flattery she gave them. At a party, one of her acquaintances asked me, "Don't you think it's a little much for a woman of her age to be dressed and acting like that?"

I replied, "I don't know her age, but I think she looks great."

Her so-called friend smiled, "She was in the

same class in school with my sister who is 66."

"She couldn't be 66!"

"Ha, I think she might be older. She's probably at least 67."

I smiled, "Whew. She sure had kept in good shape."

"She's had some help. All of her wrinkles disappeared last winter when she said she was in the Caribbean. And look at that blonde hair. You know, at her age you don't have that color. Do you think it looks natural?"

"It looks pretty good to me."

The woman continued, "Tell me this. She admits to being 58 yet she has a son on the young side of 50. You don't think she had him when she was seven, do you?"

I couldn't believe this conversation. Why was this person being so spiteful and catty. Was she jealous of Dottie? Clearly, she was.

I had to answer her about having a baby at age seven. "I thought her son was in his early forties. She could have had him when she was 16 or 17, making her 57 or 58."

Seeming a bit miffed, the grand dame murmured, "Humph, you men are all alike. You judge a book by the cover."

She walked away as I professed, "I like the cover. Not a bad book, either."

I couldn't believe that Dottie was in her mid-

60s. I wondered if the woman was right.

Later, it was confirmed that she was 67.

Dottie's personality had two sides. Charming with men, caustic with women.

My favorite encounter concerning Dottie was at a party given by a mutual friend named Sallie Bell Johnson. It was a function honoring Sallie Bell's son and his new wife, Mr. and Mrs. Malcolm Giles. He was a product of Sallie Bell's first husband, thus a different last name. Malcolm and his wife lived in Arizona and were visiting his mother for the first time since the wedding.

Dottie had to make reference to the fact that the names of mother and son were not the same. Everyone at the party knew that Sallie Bell had been married three times and had children by all three husbands. Dottie's remark annoyed Sallie Bell. Everyone noticed the tension building up between the two women.

Husband number two had been a prominent jeweler and had showered his wife with many gifts during their marriage. Her jewelry, particularly her diamonds, was well known to her friends. Sallie Bell's prize possession was a four-carat diamond ring that was flaunted at every opportunity. It was a true dazzler.

She was flashing it at her son's party and everyone was admiring how beautiful and brilliant it was. Dottie, a bit envious, made a remark to a

The Ultimate Put-down

bystander that the diamond was not a real diamond at all. "It's a fake," she mused.

Sallie Bell overheard the stinging remark and said nothing. She was still smarting over the earlier comment about her son's name. One of her friends, Frank McNeill, could feel the pressure mounting and guided Dottie into the dining room. He thought it would be wise to keep her as far as possible from their hostess. Her remarks had convinced him that there was a great amount of jealousy there. The ring was getting more attention than Dottie. She didn't like that at all. Frank kept her attention by telling her what she wanted to hear. What a knockout she was and what a super personality she had. Little was said about anything or any body else. Only Dottie. After several minutes, Sallie Bell appeared in the dining room with a few of her guests in tow. She nodded and smiled at Frank and Dottie as she reached for a plate and some food. Another guest commented on the ring and gushed how beautiful and elegant it was.

Dottie could not keep quiet about it. She nudged Frank, telling him that the diamond was genuine, a genuine fake.

Sallie Bell heard everything. She was infuriated. She called Dottie over to her.

Both were standing in front of a large antique china cabinet with glass doors.

Sallie Bell put her hand on the glass door at the top and pulled the ring all the way down to the bottom. Emblazoned on the glass was a deep gash from the top to the bottom.

Everyone in the room saw what was going on and gasped.

In a belting voice, Sallie Bell looked at Dottie, pointed to the glass door and asked, "You think a fake could do that?"

A few days later, a neighbor of Sallie Bell's told me that he saw a crew moving the china cabinet out to a repair shop.

Magic Pills

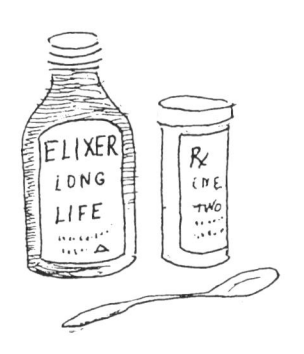

Jeremy Rhoades was born and raised on a farm near a small North Carolina town. His life was typical southern American. Public school, a few years of college, then back on the family farm. He married his high school sweetheart, Nan, and fathered two sons and two daughters.

Jeremy never remembered when people began to call him "Dusty". There were other "Dusty

Rhoades" throughout his family. It was bound to happen with a name like that.

In fact, after he first started to school, no one, including his teacher, ever referred to him as Jeremy. He grew to like his nickname of Dusty and thought it sounded friendly

As the years passed, Dusty retired from the farm and moved into a smaller house in town. His two sons took over the management of the family business. It was a wonderful situation for him and for his sons. After moving, Dusty and Nan became involved in many activities in the community. Nan started a meals on wheels program and became very busy in organizing and running a group of volunteers. Occasionally, she was forced to call on her husband for help when one of the workers was sick or on vacation.

Dusty was active in a local civic club and ended up in charge of the town's centennial celebration, the biggest happening to hit the area in many years. It was to be a weeklong event with all citizens participating in some way.

In addition to the meals on wheels and civic club activities, both Dusty and Nan were involved in their church. Nan taught Sunday school for several years, and Dusty served in many positions of leadership. They were well known in the community and had become a popular and dependable couple.

Magic Pills

When Dusty did his yard work, he always cut the grass for his next door neighbor. She was an elderly single lady and lived alone. Her name was Patricia Vance Greene, but everyone called her "Miss Pattie". She took pride in her independence. Miss Pattie was devoted to Dusty and his wife and was always taking them some homemade goodies from her kitchen. As time passed, Miss Pattie's health deteriorated but she refused to go into a retirement home, always determined to go it alone.

Eventually, the local doctor went by each day to see Miss Pattie. Dr. Roy Pryor was everybody's favorite doctor in town. He was the only doctor in town. When Dr. Roy went to see Miss Pattie, he only stayed a few minutes, but his treatment worked wonders. In no time at all, Miss Pattie was seen sweeping the front porch and steps or watering her flowers and bushes.

Dusty thought that Dr. Roy was wonderful to come by every day and perform a miracle for a sweet old lady. Dr. Roy would surely get to heaven when his time came.

Some of the townspeople suspected that Miss Pattie had become too dependent on Dr. Roy's visits. Others were convinced that she had become a drug addict. Why was it that she never appeared outside her home when Dr. Roy was away? She didn't pick up her newspaper, which was left on her front porch every morning, or even answer her telephone.

As soon as Dr. Roy returned to his daily visit, Miss Pattie reappeared as usual.

The following autumn, Dusty began to feel as if he was catching a cold. He drank a lot of water and orange juice and took a pain pill every four hours. When Nan felt his forehead, she was convinced he had a temperature. She knew he had the flu and suggested that they call Dr. Roy

Dusty thought about it for a few moments before he agreed, "I want to get well. Tell Dr.Roy to come by and bring me some of those Miss Pattie Greene pills."

Birthday Girl

My granddaughter was celebrating her 5th birthday and was planning to have a party in observance of it. She had heard the story and seen the movie of "Cinderella" and had been completely mesmerized by it. For her birthday party, it was natural that she picked a Cinderella theme for it. Her father and mother had intended to have an outdoor picnic in their backyard. They had a list of children who had invited their daughter to their homes for birthday events, and it was pay back time.

Their yard would definitely be identified as a home with small children. A swing set, sand-box, a small trampoline, and picnic tables with built-in seats. It was obvious who lived there.

As the eventful day approached, the birthday girl got a bit more excited. Invitations had been mailed earlier so all of her friends were talking to her about coming and what costume they were intending to wear. She was planning her outfit from head to toe and organizing every detail of it. After all, she was going to be the real Cinderella.

Her parents were kept busy getting the decorations in order and planning the refreshments. Everything was being coordinated so that the party would run smoothly and be a big success. Since it was to be outside, they had to make alternative plans in case of bad weather. They had thought of everything.

On the day of the party, the backyard was decorated with colorful balloons, posters of the fairy tale and two large mirrors, the kind that are attached to the back of a bedroom door. They were tied to trees, standing at ground lever and ran up the trunk about five feet. The idea was for each of the participants at the party to look at his or her costume and to preen a bit. After all, dressing up was a big part of growing up.

At the party, I approached my granddaughter as she was primping in front of one of the mirrors. I called her by name, but she didn't answer. She turned and said, "I'm Cinderella. Please call me by my real name."

She was Cinderella, period. She was dressed for the ball in a long blue formal gown. Her long hair was pulled back and held in place by a headband, showing off her big gold and pearl earrings. She wore a black ribbon around her neck with a big pearl at her throat. She was wearing make-up on both cheeks and bright red lipstick. The crowning part of the costume was her long white gloves that ran from above her elbow to four inches below her fingertips. They were overlapping her hands. Her fingers were up in the gloves. It was truly a fantastic sight. She looked like a princess. It made me chuckle to see her looking like a grown up in those flapping long gloves.

The refreshments were also in keeping with the Cinderella motif. In the center of the blue iced cake was a doll about 18 inches tall, making it look like Cinderella in a fancy dress ball gown, hoop skirt and all. The rest of the goodies were color coordinated with the cake.

When the other children arrived in their costumes, there was much squealing and laughing. No one came as Cinderella. I don't think they wanted to compete with their hostess. Three different boys came as the prince and twin brothers came as mice. A beautiful blonde girl dressed as the fairy godmother with her magic wand. Her younger sister came as a pumpkin. It was clever in keeping with the party theme and also usable for a Halloween outfit. Nobody dressed as the wicked stepmother or as the two ugly stepsisters.

Two weeks before the party, her father was putting the birthday girl to bed one evening. In order to lull her to sleep, he told her about the plans for the party. Since it was going to be her special day, she listened intently as he talked about it. He speculated what her friends were going to wear. Would any come without a costume? And how about the boys. What would they come as?

The conversation went on for several minutes before my son told her that my wife and I were coming and that I was going to wear a tuxedo.

She smiled and said, "That's wonderful."

Then, her father told her about both of her other grandparents who were coming from out of town. She was pleased to hear that.

Then it was time for her to go to sleep. But, she had one more question.

"You said that Grandfather was coming and wearing a tuxedo."

"That's right, he is."

The would-be Cinderella frowned and asked, "Daddy, what's a tuxedo?"

Mama's Politics

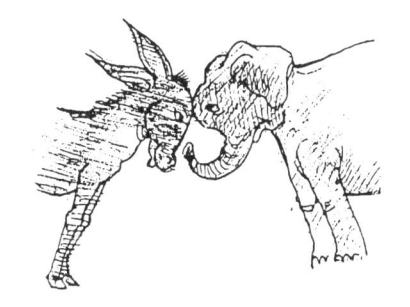

My grandfather, who died before I was born, was a congressman from North Carolina. . Naturally, I never knew him, but there isn't a story about him that I haven't heard. According to my mother, he was one of the greatest mortals who ever lived. His children called him "Poppa" and he and my grandmother had a brood of eight. Six lived to ripe old ages, including my mother.

When I was young, I never thought much about

members of my family having such great paying government jobs. One of my uncles was the local postmaster for many years. An older cousin had a high level Federal job in Washington and several other relatives were on the government payroll. As I got older and smarter, I felt my grandfather's influence and patronage flowing through the generations. While I was growing up, it seemed that it lasted a long time, but then came the Republicans. Poppa had been a loyal and staunch Democrat.

Over the years, most of the family members had embraced the Democrat party. Many were quite active in the local political scene and some even held positions in the state hierarchy. With our grandfather's ghostly influence, it was no mystery as to why. Some affectionately called themselves "yellow dog democrats,"

There were, however, a few who left the fold later in life and became Republicans. I was one of them.

This wasn't a sudden thing. It didn't happen until I was married, had children and started my own business. I became active in the local Republican committee and worked within the party framework and in local, state and national elections. It was something I enjoyed doing.

After a few years, I decided to run for the state legislature. It was a citywide race to elect five members at large for the Virginia House of Delegates. There were already five Democrat incumbents filling those seats. In our party convention, we had only two candidates for the nomination. Both of the two were chosen and I was one of them.

By that time, I had gotten to know all of the activists in the committee and had received their encouragement and support. The campaign was not going to be easy and I was depending on them for their help.

At that time, my mother was 91 years old and living in a nursing home. Her mind was good for her age; her physical condition was not. She needed nursing care.

When I went to see her to tell about my becoming a certified candidate for office, she was thrilled.

Her first reaction was, "You'll be the best Democrat in Washington."

I responded, "Mother, this not Congress. This is not Washington, but the State Legislature in Richmond,"

"Well, then, you'll be the best Democrat in Richmond."

"Something else, Mother. I'm not a Democrat."
She looked puzzled.
I continued, "I'm a Republican"
"When did this happen?" she quizzed.

"Several years ago, I joined the Republican party committee."

She was frowning. I thought maybe that I should not have told her. It was cruel to shock her like that. I knew how important being a Democrat was to her. She had such wonderful memories of her father and of the times she had spent with him particularly in Washington when she was young and he was in Congress.

She had always taught me to tell the truth when I was growing up, no matter how bad it hurt.

Still frowning, she remarked, "I love you, but I can't vote for you."

"But, Mother. I was going to get you an absentee ballot."

I tried to explain to her that the philosophy of the Democrat party had changed considerably over the years.

Continuing, I said, "It's not the same party that Poppa represented. If he were living today, he would probably be a Republican."

She had been lying in bed all during our conversation, but sat up abruptly, looked me in the eye, and declared, "Do not desecrate your grandfather's memory. He was a true and loyal Democrat. He was not a turncoat and would never be one."

I got her message loud and clear. I thought I had better end my visit and move out of her room. I

Mama's Politics

leaned over and kissed her goodbye and left.

She was mumbling, "I can't believe it. I can't believe my son is a Republican. Where or where did I go wrong?"

A few days later, I visited her again. She told me that several of her nursing home buddies wanted my bumper sticker. Two residents wanted to register to vote and many more wanted absentee ballots. I thought they were going to vote for me, but then I found out they were all Democrats. Even though they had my posters hanging over their beds and my bumper sticker on their wheelchairs, they were voting for my opponent. No wonder the Democrats did so well with such aggressive, loyal and interested workers.

Before the election, my political brochures and position statements had invaded the home. I enjoyed going there since everyone treated me like I was a celebrity.

As it turned out, I came in 6th in the election. All Democrats were re-elected. To put it another way, I came in number one of the two Republicans. That sounded better than coming in 6th.

My mother did not vote. If she had done so and voted for me, I still would not have won. I needed a lot more than her one vote.

She died the next year. At her funeral, I thought about her leaving this world with great satisfaction. She could tell her Poppa that in her 92 years on earth, she never voted Republican.

A few years later, I ran again and won. My two opponents never knew that my own mother would not vote for me. If they found out, what a field day that would have been! I can see and hear the political advertisements now:

"His own Mother wouldn't vote for him. Listen to her – don't vote for him.

Vote for me!"

Buck & Sally

My grandfather had a sister named Sally who was married to a man called Buck. My grandfather always called her "Sister", never by her given name. Her husband called her "Sally". Since Sally was my father's aunt, it would have been appropriate to call her "Aunt Sally", but no. Since she was called "Sister" by her brother, and "Sally" by others, someone started calling her "Sister Sally". It stuck. All of the family including my age group of nieces, nephews and cousins addressed her as "Sister Sally," Uncle Buck and Sister Sally were a unique couple. They were devoted to one another, but each had a mind of their own. He was older by 19 years. When they were married, he was 40 and she was 21. It never occurred to me that they were of two different generations. Their personalities were somewhat opposite. He was reserved and quiet. She was outgoing and never lost for words. However, their characters and values were the same.

Their lifestyle was formal and old fashioned Victorian. It was understandable since both had been born in the latter part of the 19th century. They were not wealthy but lived such a refined and genteel existence that one might think of them as "old money." Their home was tastefully furnished with heirlooms that had been passed down through the families. It was a wonderful place to visit. It always gave me such a warm feeling to be there.

Uncle Buck and Sister Sally had four children of their own. All were in the same age group as my father. Even though I was not the same era, I always felt very close to that part of the family.

A few years before Uncle Buck passed away, Sister Sally had planned a big family reunion at their home. They had lived there ever since they were married. It was a big country style house in the middle of a small Virginia town.

Sister Sally was working out a sleeping plan for each member of the clan. She envisioned that one family unit could take over a complete bedroom, using the regular bed, rollaways and sleeping bags for the children. That was no problem.

The dilemma was that there were several individuals and couples with no children who would be attending. Even though they were kinfolk, their spouses were not. It would be awkward to place them together for sleeping purposes.

Sister Sally had a great idea. She would separate them by gender. One room for the women and one room for the men. She decided to turn the master bedroom into one of the dormitories, which meant that she and Uncle Buck had to separate. She asked him about it.

He told her, "Sally, I don't care what you arrange or where you place me, but remember that there are two things I don't do."

She asked, "Two things? What are they, Buck?"

"I don't sleep with any live man," then paused before continuing, "or any dead woman."

Sister Sally giggled, "I needed a laugh. I'm a bit uptight trying to place everyone in the right sleeping place.

The reunion was a big success and everyone

Funny Bone

agreed that it should become an annual event. Uncle Buck was not very enthused about having to give up his bedroom. Once was one time too many as far as he was concerned.

After Uncle Buck entered the world of retirement, he joined a group of his friends at the local downtown restaurant each weekday morning for coffee and conversation. It was almost a ritual with him and the others. It got them out of the house and out of the way of their wives.

One day, Uncle Buck was standing outside the restaurant, talking to his friend, Wade. Two rather overweight women were walking on the other side of the street and waved to the two men.

Uncle Buck asked Wade, "Who is that swallow tailed woman over there?"

Wade, who had a slight speech impediment, replied, "That's my thister Franthes."

Uncle Buck was somewhat taken back by his insensitive remark. He thought quickly that he should redeem himself, saying, "Oh, not Frances, I know her. I mean the other one."

Wade responded, "Oh, that's my other thister Dodie."

Uncle Buck thought that this was not going to be his best day.

Uncle Buck and Sister Sally were a wonderful pair. He lived until he was 92 years old, but Sister Sally made it to 99. She was bright and spunky right to the end.

When Sister Sally was 94, everyone in the family got together for a family wedding. After the rehearsal dinner, a group was sitting around when the matriarch exclaimed that she had some wonderful news to tell. All of her four children and their husbands and wives were there, anxiously waiting to hear what she had to say.

She announced, "Last week, I got my drivers license renewed. Isn't that wonderful?"

Sister Sally's oldest daughter blurted out, "Mother, I've been praying that you wouldn't get it."

Sister Sally cut her big brown eyes at her daughter and boasted, "And, I've been praying I would."

We all got the unspoken message of who had the best line of communication with the Almighty. Sister Sally kept on smiling.

One of her sons asked, "Didn't they know that you were 94 years old?"

"Of course, he did. My date of birth in on the license."

Her son continued, "Did he suggest that you not drive anymore?"

"He mentioned it, but I told him that I wouldn't drive at night, only in the daytime."

Sister Sally persisted, "And, I only would drive to five places."

Funny Bone

"And where were those five places?" she was quizzed.

Holding up her right hand, she rattled off the different places, touching a finger after naming each.

"I told him I drove to church," striking finger number one.

"To the post office," striking number two.

"To the market," touching number three.

"To the beauty parlor," tapping number four.

And grabbing her thumb for number five, "When my children come to visit, I drive to the whiskey store."

We all agreed that the motor vehicle inspector who renewed her license had met an artist. Con artist, that is.

Today, whenever I think of Uncle Buck and Sister Sally, there is always a big smile on my face.

Sunny Eyes

I decided to throw my hat into the political arena and to run for a seat in the state legislature. First, it was necessary to get nominated as a candidate by my political party. Since there was not to be a primary election, the decision was to be made by a caucus or a convention.

I had been active in the local political committee for several years, working from the lowest job to chairman. I knew most the people who would be attending the caucus. They were receptive to my running and promised their support for my candidacy. I won the nomination and became a full-fledged candidate.

After receiving the nomination, I had to run in the general election against the candidate of the other political party. There would only be the two of us and the election was to be held in three and a half months.

There were other people running for offices other than the state legislature during the same election. It was going to be an interesting and busy three months.

Campaigning was a new and exciting experience for me. Being a novice opened my eyes to many aspects of the political world. The name of the game was to get people to vote for you. That was the ultimate goal. Not only was getting the commitment to support critical, also important was getting the voter to actively go to the polls on Election Day. Promises to vote for you were significant, but if one did not go and actually vote, the promise was ineffective.

I learned that in order to get support, one had to communicate with the voter. Personal contact was the most important aspect of campaigning. People were interested in your political philosophy and, more importantly, what you thought about specific matters that interested them. Personal contact and the "pressing the flesh" were high on the list of the campaign plan.

Other strategic methods of communicating were through direct mailing of letters, newspaper, radio and television advertisements, bumper stickers, yard signs and public forums. These cost money. Raising funds was not an easy job, especially if this was a first run. A budget for the entire campaign was necessary. With financing in the forefront of any planning, the decisions of the what, when and wherefores were made. Then, it was necessary to visit prominent leaders in the community and seek their support. Endorsements by elected officials, as well as popular citizens and organizations, would enhance one's candidacy and give the candidate some creditability with the voters.

During the campaign, the demand on your time is unbelievable. Never pass up an opportunity to meet voters or to get your name out to the public. Name identification is a must.

A successful local politician met with me and gave me some sage advice. Never say "me". That is a no-no in the political game. "Vote for me." When voters go into the voting booth, there is no "me" listed. Always say your last name when you ask for a vote. That is the name that will be at the voting booth. Name identification again.

He also gave me a few pointers on how to state

Funny Bone

my name when talking without sounding foolish or obvious. Politicians know all the rules and the tools of the trade in promoting their names and images.

A few weeks before the election, I was invited to attend a day in the park with the other office seekers. We were expected to mix with the crowd during the afternoon until 4:30 at which time we were all introduced to the gathering. Each candidate was to say a few words, not to exceed three minutes. With several people speaking, it could take too much time. Three minutes was not much time to be serious, particularly at a party of revelers.

By late afternoon, I don't think it made too much difference what was said. The crowd had been partying for several hours and were not too anxious to participate in a solemn dialogue. Forget issues. Just don't say anything stupid or make a fool of yourself. Smile and wave. It's what they wanted.

My son went with me, not only for moral support, but also as aide-de-camp. He was to assist me when needed. Sometimes it is difficult for a candidate who is working the crowd to do many things that one would take for granted. Just getting a drink of water can be a problem. Normally, it is best not to eat until later when contacting potential voters. Besides, it is a bit rude to discuss a political question with a mouth full of food.

My son and I settled on a signal for him to come to my rescue if I got hooked up with someone I couldn't leave gracefully. He would come over and say that I was needed at another location. Our plan was for me to take off my eyeglasses and wipe them with my handkerchief. When he saw the signal, he was to approach me immediately and relieve the situation.

With that in mind, junior was to stay fairly close by and keep his eye on me at all times, particularly when I was engaged in a long conversation with others.

During the afternoon, an older woman came up to me and asked what I thought about a specific issue. When I told her of my thoughts on it, she agreed. We were together on it. I thought that I had scored with her, but she had to go into greater detail with the pros and cons of the issue. She went on and on about it, explaining every detail. After several minutes, I decided I had better alert my son to come to the rescue.

I kept nodding my head in agreement and took out my handkerchief. When I started wiping my glasses, I glanced at my son. He was in a lively conversation with an attractive young lady. He looked at me for a few seconds, noticing that I was cleaning my glasses. Nevertheless, he continued talking with the young lady, completely ignoring my signal.

Another few minutes of listening to the lady rant on about the same subject, I put my glasses back on. I glanced over and waited for my son to look at me. Finally, his eyes met mine. I immediately took off my glasses, reached for my handkerchief and started cleaning them again. I was completely disregarded for the second time.

The lady asked me, "Do you have an eye problem or are your glasses bothering you?"

I responded, "Neither, I'm having trouble with my son,"

She nodded at me, "I can understand. It's just too bright. You should always wear sunglasses when you are out in the sun."

Sweet and Sour

Tommy was a tough guy, and as they used to say, rough as pig iron. The first time I saw him, he was shirtless on a hot summer day, painting an old wooden chair. He had separated from his wife and was living temporarily with his mother who lived in an apartment building which I managed. We introduced ourselves to one another and made some chitchat. I noticed he had several tattoos on parts of his body. Two in particular caught my eye.

One was over his right breast marked "Sweet" and the other over his left imprinted "Sour". I thought to myself that this character was something else.

As time passed, we referred to Tommy as "Sweet and Sour". Of course, we never called him that so he could hear it. Everyone who knew him had no doubt to whom we were referring when we used his nickname.

In addition to the tattoos on his chest, he had one on his left bicep that read "In memory of my mother". That one puzzled me a lot since I knew his mother, and she was very much alive.

When I got to know Sweet and Sour better, I asked him why his tattoo was in memory of his mother rather than in honor of her.

He responded, "Oh, I got that one when I was drunk one night. The guy didn't know that Mama was still living."

On his right hand, each finger had a letter tattooed on it between the joint and the knuckle. It read "L-O-V-E".

Tommy had a full time job at a local tobacco factory, but was always doing odd jobs, some for pay and some as favors. He could do almost anything and did them quite well. He helped me out many times in my real estate business, working on weekends and at night.

Several months after our meeting, I sold several apartment buildings which I began to manage. I called on Tommy a few times to do some small repair jobs which he did very professionally and charged little. In a very short time, I recognized that he took great pride in his work and wanted to please his customers. A compliment to him for a job well done was just as important as the pay he received.

Here was a street-wise guy who was almost obsessed with being the ultimate virile man, but had a wide, sensitive streak underneath that tough exterior. A little flattery went a long way with him.

Tommy got into an argument with his boss at the tobacco factory, ending up in a physical altercation. He quit his job. He was to tell me about it, but insisted that what he did was not wrong.

"No dingbat is going to tell me I don't know what I'm doing," he lamented. "If anybody don't know what he's doing, it was him, not me."

It was obviously clear that his boss had hurt his pride. The physical skirmish was bad to have happened, but it was hurt feelings that caused him to leave. I tried to get him to think twice about quitting his job, but my efforts were to no avail. He would never apologize. He had too much pride.

Tommy wanted me to give him more jobs. He said he wished that I had enough work to keep him

Funny Bone

busy all the time.

As it turned out, my management business was growing, but did not need a regular maintenance person. We worked out a plan that Tommy would be responsible for all my requirements as well as take other odd jobs that came along. The only problem was with emergencies, when other help had to be used. We worked together under those conditions for a few months until it developed into a full time job for him.

We worked well together for several years. He remarried and moved his new bride into his mother's apartment. I thought this was big mistake but I was wrong. It turned out to be one big happy family.

Tommy and I got along fine. Even though we were employer and employee, we became friends. I understood him, rough on the outside, but a pussycat on the inside. He always called me "Bossman" which I never really liked. But, he got a kick out of it, so I accepted it. He enjoyed telling people that I was his bossman.

Tommy came into my office one day and told me he wanted to talk about a situation that had occurred the day before. One of the owners of a company doing business with us had offered him a job, trying to lure him away.

He did not like it. He thought the man was doing something underhanded to me and felt that he would not like to work for anyone with such an obvious character flaw. The businessman had gotten to know Tommy only through his work with my company. I told him that I appreciated his telling me about it and of his loyalty to me. He remarked that it was a two-way street, that I had always been loyal to him. Needless to say, that conversation cemented our relationship.

When he was younger, Tommy's family lived in a rough neighborhood. After his father's death, he was thrust into the adult world. He became a tough teenager and learned the facts of life the hard way. His masculine image was necessary to deal with his fellow ruffian friends. Any deviation from their standard was classified as sissy. It was their way, or no way.

Knowing his background, I tried to make him understand that everyone was different. Not everyone wanted to be like him or like me. I hope he understood what I was trying to tell him. Accept people as they are, not what you want them to be.

I recall one incident in which I challenged his tough, manly image. I had bought a man's black umbrella and kept it in my car in case I got caught in the rain.

One cloudy and threatening day, I took the umbrella out of the car. As I walked across the street to meet Tommy, he asked, "What the heck is that?"

"What it looks like. An umbrella," I said.

"Why are you carrying it?"

A little irked, I answered, "Because I don't want to get wet if it rains."

Tommy kept on, "You ain't sugar. You think you're gonna melt?"

"I don't want to get wet and catch a cold."

Tommy shook his head and mumbled something I couldn't understand.

We checked out the property and determined what work had to be done. As I walked to the car, I realized that I had left my umbrella on the porch of the building. Before I could get back to it, Tommy hollered, "Hey, Bossman, you forgot your parasol."

Driving back to the office, I vowed that I'd never open that umbrella again around Mister Sweet and Sour. "Your parasol". I got his message loud and clear.

American Mother

During World War II, I had been drafted into the Army right out of college. The timing was perfect since I received my induction notice weeks before final exams. Naturally, I was not qualified to finish my classes so I lost about a third of my junior semester. My father was very concerned that he would not receive any refund for my less than full time attendance and that he would be shortchanged for it. There was no doubt that he was correct in his assumption.

After the war was over, I went back to school under the GI bill so my parents had no reason to fight the school from my earlier experience. It didn't bother me, but my father still thought he was due a refund.

After entering the Army. I was tested thoroughly by the military and was told that I had language ability, whatever that was. After completing basic training, further testing of me would be done and it was possible that I would be able to continue my education while still in the service, but only in a language program.

After spending twelve weeks in a stripped down St. Petersburg, Florida luxury hotel taken over by the United States military, I completed my initial training. Then, I was sent to a Colorado school, which was not an armed forces installation. I was tested for my language ability, both written and orally, and passed. I had taken two years of beginning Spanish prior to my entrance into the Army, so studying a foreign language was a fairly recent experience for me.

After the testing, I was sent with a small group to the University of Wisconsin in Madison to begin my Spanish language course. We arrived there during the last week of August and were settled in a fraternity house, which had closed down for the war. All of us were in the active Army. We waited for classes to begin the middle of September. For the three week waiting period, we attended to our soldier duties and were kept busy as gardeners, cutting the grass on campus, trimming shrubbery, pulling up weeds, and anything else that needed attention.

At that time of the year, the weather in Madison was perfect. It was pleasantly warm during the day and cool at night. Little did I realize in early September that old man winter would arrive within the next several weeks, bringing the coldest climate I had ever encountered. Up to that time, my life had been spent in the South and I was not used to Wisconsin winters. Even the Army had sent me to Florida for basic training during the previous winter months and then to Colorado for the summer. I was getting spoiled by being in the right place at the right time.

The last week before classes began at the university; we were all given three-day passes. A few of us went to Chicago on the train. Chicago was the greatest place in the world to be if you were in the military during World War II. The whole city and its people opened up their hearts and pocketbooks and made us all feel appreciated and loved. We all looked forward to spending a few days in the Windy City.

On Sunday night, after such a terrific time in

Chicago, I returned to my quarters in Madison, only to be told that I had been moved to a different fraternity house at another location. Without any prior notice, all of my belongings had been taken to my new home. I didn't like the idea that they had the authority to do that without contacting me first. But, this was the army.

When I arrived at the new place, I was met by a civilian who greeted me with, *"Buona Sera"*. I asked in English if this were the correct place for me. He wasn't speaking Spanish but some other language. Spanish was what I was supposed to be studying there.

He responded, *"No English, solo italiano."*

I understood. "No English, only Italian."

I replied in Spanish, *"Soy en el espanol classe, no italiano."* (I'm in Spanish class, not Italian.)

He understood what I said and showed me a list of names that had moved into the house, and there was mine. I knew it was a big mistake but I resolved that it was too late on a Sunday night to do anything about it. I agreed to stay there overnight and get everything corrected the next morning.

"Manana", I said.

"Domani, va bene", the civilian replied.

The next day, I only heard Italian spoken. All the American soldiers were speaking it. I tried to speak English to them but was told one could only communicate in the Italian language. If you did not know the word, you looked it up in the English-Italian dictionary.

Later that morning, I met with the official Army commander of the school and was told that the military needed Italian interpreters, not Spanish translators. I had been selected for the program since I had tested well for my language ability and because I was not of Italian lineage. The military did not want anyone with any Italian connections to become involved since Italy was not our ally at the time.

Our conversation was in English. However, I was instructed to speak only Italian in class, our quarters and at meals.

After nine months of extensive study in Italian vocabulary, grammar, history and geography, I was sent to a camp in Alabama to join a group of Italian prisoners of war who had been brought to America from North Africa. While I had been in school, Italy had changed from being aligned with the Axis, the enemy of America, to becoming a co-belligerent, as part of the Allied group. In other words, Italy had joined our team.

I lived and worked with the Italian soldiers for the next two years until the end of the war. They worked at various jobs throughout the military establishment especially in the quartermaster supply and repair departments. Some even worked

Funny Bone

in the different service clubs, recreation facilities and theaters. None were allowed in critical or sensitive programs.

Prisoners of war received $24 per month for extra personal living expenses, according to the Geneva Convention. Most of the soldiers withdrew from $12 to $15 per month for spending money and saved the difference. Each had an account for their savings.

After Victory Europe (VE) day in May, 1945, the Italians knew that they would be going home in the near future. They began buying gifts with their savings to take to their families, then, after Victory Japan (VJ) day in August 1945, the deluge of buying began. Every weekend, the Italians were permitted to go into town to shop along with an American military interpreter. They were not allowed to go alone.

Since I had bought an old Model A Ford roadster, I would take three people out for shopping. My first adventure was a disaster, since I took four Italians, two in the front with me and two in the rumble seat. The only problem with that was there was no room for their purchases with five in the car. After that, I limited it to four including me. I became very popular because of my car and also could communicate with them in their native tongue. Some of the soldiers were able to speak English to a point, but others could only say a few phrases.

The Italian POWs wore a basic American uniform with plain, solid buttons. No. U.S. insignia and no rank or grade designation. Instead, on the sleeve of their jacket or shirt was an oval, bright green patch at least six inches wide with the word "ITALY" adorned in white. Their caps and hats contained a round green, white and red patch with "ITALY" embroidered in the center. It was very visible and clear that these men were Italians, not Americans.

One afternoon, I took three Italians into a department store. The were very interested in purchasing bolts of cloth to take home so that their families could sew and make all kinds of wearing apparel. It was difficult for them to understand our system of inches, feet and yards, since they were used to the metric system. I explained the different measurements as best I could to them, speaking in Italian. Then I would order for them in English in my southern accent to the saleslady. After giving several orders and conferring with the foreign soldiers in their native tongue, then speaking in English, the saleslady remarked, "You certainly do speak good English."

Before responding, I thought for a minute. Can't she see that I am an American? I was wearing a United States Army uniform with U.S. insignia, shiny brass buttons, and a unit patch as well as my

Funny Bone

corporal stripes on my sleeve. There were no "ITALY" patches on my jacket or my cap.

Ringing in my ears, "you certainly do speak good English", I nodded by head up and down and acknowledged her remark.

"Thank you. My mother is an American."

Her comeback, "Oh, no wonder."

The Football Dilemma

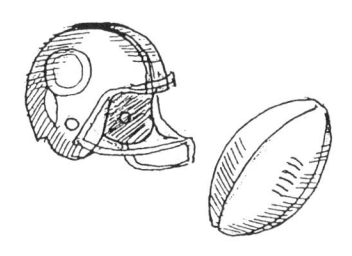

The telephone rang in my bedroom at home before seven o'clock on a Sunday morning in mid December.

"Hello", I answered after being jolted out of a deep sleep. I wondered who could be calling at this hour.

The voice on the other end was enthusiastic and upbeat.

"This is Harry Barker and I apologize for calling

you so early. I have two tickets for the Redskins football game today in Washington and I can't use them. I know you're a fan and thought that you might like to go. I know that this is short notice, but would you like them?"

Getting my wits together at that hour, I replied, "Sure, that's super. Thank you very much for thinking of me."

My positive response was natural. Being in the real estate business, I had learned long ago to always answer "yes" immediately. If a client asked if I wanted to place a for sale or for rent sign on the listed property, it was always affirmative. One should never hesitate. You can always change your mind later. It's much easier changing from a yes to a no than the other way around.

At the moment of the telephone call and in my half sleep, I did not even know what my plans were for the day other than attending church services. I knew that if I could not go to the game, there were a number of friends who would grab the opportunity. Redskins home game tickets were very popular and generally difficult, if not impossible to obtain. This was an offer of the greatest magnitude.

Harry Barker was not what I would call a friend, but an acquaintance that I had known for many years and helped in the past. On one particular occasion, his wife had car trouble in front of my

The Football Dilemma

office. She did not know what to do and came into my building to use the telephone. Her trouble was a leaking radiator hose and she was very upset about it. When she raised the hood of the car, she was baffled by the steam coming from the motor. It caught her by surprise. She thought the engine was going to blow up.

I went out to see what had happened and tried to calm her down. After I saw what the problem was, I did a quick patch with some duct tape after things had cooled down a bit. With the engine on, I poured some water in the radiator and sent her on her way.

Harry called me that evening and told me how much he and his wife appreciated my kindness and help. His wife was so glad to see my familiar face when she walked into my office. He also promised that he would never forget my good deed to them. When he offered me the tickets to the football game, his words of not forgetting me came to mind. I'm glad he remembered. He was a man of his word.

Our homes were in different parts of the city and several miles apart. We arranged to meet at a convenient location about half way for each within the hour before Harry left town. His wife's father had suffered a heart attack the day before and was doing fine. They were going to see him as well as give her mother some moral support. He was being well taken care of in the hospital, but her mother needed her family there.

I thought about my plans for the day and decided that I would skip church and put off some chores I intended to do that afternoon for later on the following week. I really wanted to go to the game but my wife was not at all interested in it. I thought of numerous people to ask before selecting my oldest son who was having a birthday in a few days. He was married with a family of his own, so I thought I had better call him as soon as possible in case he could not go. All of his life, he had complained that he had been cheated since he was born so near to Christmas. Growing up, he would receive a combination present for his birthday and Christmas, especially on big items. He felt that he got gypped since his brother and sisters fared better with separate gifts for each occasion. I thought that a trip to the Redskins game would be an extra bonus for him.

Before I left the house to pick up the tickets, I telephoned and told him about my plans. He was very interested in what I was saying about going. This would be an added special treat to honor his birthday.

" If you can work it in, would you like to go with me?" I asked.

His response was, "Where did you get the tickets?"

The Football Dilemma

I retorted, "The answer to my question is a yes or a no."

He replied, "Yes, yes, yes."

He still wanted to know the whole story of how I got the tickets.

Then I told him what really happened as well as the scenario for the day. It was a little more than a two-hour drive from our city to the nation's capital, so we arranged to leave at least three hours before kickoff time. We wanted to allow some extra time in case we ran into some traffic slow downs on the highway and in parking at the stadium.. We definitely wanted to be there at the very beginning of the game.

It was a cold day and had snowed north of Richmond that week. We hardly ever received any of the white stuff. Richmond is not in the snow belt that runs about half way to Charlottesville to the west and around Fredericksburg to the north. We do get some snow but not like those on the other side of the imaginary belt line.

My son and I met and headed for the interstate highway. A lot of talk about how wonderful it was to be going, how great Harry Baker was to give us the tickets and what a terrific birthday surprise for both the giver and receiver. It was going to be an unforgettable day.

About forty five minutes after we left home, my son asked me, "Dad, when we get there, suppose someone offered you $100 for your ticket, would you sell it?"

"I don't think so, son."

He continued, "I'd have to take it. After all, Christmas is the week after next and I could use the money. I'd like to see the game, but I don't think it's worth $100 to me."

He had three children, all less than seven years of age and a wife. I knew what he meant about the money. I had been there myself when he was much younger.

I told him that the game would not be broadcast in the District area so there was no way for us to see it on television anywhere in Washington. I had high hopes of being there and seeing it. It had been four years since I had been to a Redskins home game. I was a big fan and really wanted to see the live action. The money would be excellent but it was worth $100 to me not to sell my ticket.

I inquired, "Do you think anybody would pay $100 on a snowy day?"

He thought a moment and came back with, "It's not snowing now."

We drove on for a few more miles, neither one speaking.

I was thinking that I should think about him and not myself. Was I being selfish? After all, it was his birthday. Christmas was so near. I wanted to go to the game, but I also wanted to do right by

The Football Dilemma

him. I was ready to say that I would sell my ticket for $100. Before I could get the words out of my mouth, he spoke.

"How about $150?"

"I'll do what you want to do. If you want to sell for $100, go ahead and do it. Include me in the deal, too. I don't want to be the grinch that ruined Christmas."

He smiled, "Thanks. Thanks, a lot. You don't know how much I appreciate that."

I thought if I sold my ticket, what would I tell Harry Barker? He gave them to me in good faith and here I was selling them at scalper's prices and not going to the game. I rationalized the situation and hoped he would understand that I did it for my son. And, maybe I should give him the money that I got for my one ticket.

The more we drove north, the evidence of the snow became apparent. The highway had been cleared and was fine for driving but there were white patches on the ground until finally the entire land area was covered with the white melting snow.

When we arrived at the stadium, the parking lot was a sea of mud mixed with white caps of snow. It was a big mess. As soon as we got out of the car, people were holding available tickets above their heads, hawking, "Need a ticket? Need a ticket?"

Funny Bone

I walked over in the muddy field to one potential seller and asked how much he wanted for his ticket.

He shouted, "Twenty dollar tickets for a bargain, only ten dollars. Half price. Only ten dollars."

I looked at my son. He looked at me. We both laughed.

"Happy birthday!"

Value of a Dollar

As a fiscal conservative, I have always tried to teach my children the value of a dollar. It still irks me to hear someone say, "It only costs a dollar." Even worse, I actually cringe when I hear a television ad hawking an exceptional buy for a specific auto for only $20,000. Twenty thousand dollars should never be referred to as "only". It is still a great deal of money in my book.

I grew up during the great depression of the

1930's. In those days, we could buy three pieces of candy for one penny. A single dip ice cream cone cost a nickel as did a bottle of soda pop. I even remember billboards in the early 1940's offering a brand new four-door Oldsmobile sedan for $777. So, with that background, I have been ingrained with what I call the depression syndrome. It simply means that I don't mind spending money, I just don't want to waste it.

My daughter Susan was planning to return to college as a sophomore and was interested in having an automobile on campus. She was not allowed to have one as freshman. During the summer after her first year, she had acquired a temporary job and had bought her brother's car which was ready for the junkyard. She realized that and made a decision on taking all of her savings to purchase a newer and more modern vehicle. She already had a buyer for the car she was presently driving, so she knew how much she could pay for her new car. Of course, the budget was not enough for a brand new one, but adequate for a good used one that would be dependable transportation.

She visited several used car dealer lots and gleaned the newspaper ads. She found a few which were in her price range. She asked me to go with her since she knew nothing about negotiating for the purchase or how to determine its mechanical condition. In asking me, she made a wise decision. Then, I realized that if she came up short of the price, she might need some financial help. That was a smart move on her part.

After looking at numerous older sporty models, which never appealed to her, we arranged to look at more traditional cars. Finally, we found one that was somewhat acceptable. She liked the robin's egg blue color, the low mileage and the price. She was reluctant to make an offer since she considered it too traditional. She even commented that it looked like an old lady's car. It would not fit her image as a with-it college student.

I explained that it was a fine, substantial automobile that would give her good service and excellent transportation until she graduated in three years. She liked it but was still sensitive that it was not sporty enough for her friends. I suggested that she drive it by her two brothers' houses to see what they thought of it. I knew that she would value their opinion since they both were interested in cars. They were a few years older, had finished college and were working.

Susan did not want me to go with her, thinking that I would influence my sons for her to buy it. She dropped me off at my home after saying that she like the way it drove. She had fiddled with every knob and switch, turning the radio on and off, raising and lowering the windows, testing the lights, blowing the horn and testing the heater and air conditioning unit.

About an hour later, she came back to say she was going to buy the car. Her brothers had both been impressed with it and told her it would be a fabulous college car. It was big enough for six passengers and had a very large trunk for lots of baggage.

It was a mid-sized car, somewhat heavy, and appeared to me to be safer than the smaller cars. It was an eight-cylinder model and would not get the best gas mileage, however, the safety factor was more important than the fuel consumption.

She bought the automobile and planned on driving it back to college in September. Before she left home, we had a long talk. I explained that she had bought the car with her own money. There were going to be expenses other than filling up the gas tank. Licenses, insurance, oil changes, repairs and new tires later on were just a few. Therefore, she should not take her friends around and just split the cost of gasoline. She was not being fair to herself. I suggested that she set a price for each person based on the miles to her destination. One dollar each to go here, a dollar and half to go there, and so on. After all, she was attending an all girls' college, which was no more than an hour away from three large coed universities. What with the football and basketball games, fraternity parties and other social activities, transportation to and from the events was important. It was also an opportunity to recoup some of the expenses and hidden costs. When Susan came home for a visit some weeks later, she told me that the car was a moneymaker. Someone had told her that if she charged a flat fee, she would be considered a business operator and would have to be licensed. Instead, she could suggest to the rider that they make a contribution for expenses. She contacted the local bus station and found out the fares to some popular destinations. She never suggested an amount of the donation, but did quote the specific cost for a one way and round trip bus ticket.

I was surprised when she told me of a trip to a college homecoming around 100 miles from her school. She loaded five people in the back and three in the front including herself. With seven contributors, she paid for the gasoline and pocketed just under $100. I remarked that eight people were far too many for the car. It was not safe to drive a long distance with that many. She informed me that she had turned down three others who wanted to go, but had seriously considered squeezing one more in the front seat. I was afraid to ask what was the largest number that she had ever transported at one time. Better I didn't know.

It finally dawned on me that my daughter was

learning some basic business principles and hopefully the value of a dollar.

I gave her a lecture about being a responsible person not only to others but to herself as well. Limit the occupancy to not more than six, including her.

Since she finished college, a new law has gone into effect in Virginia that limits the number of passengers allowed in cars driven by those under 21 years of age.

I would have voted for it.

Mall Walk

Every morning with the exception of Sunday, a number of senior citizens gather together at a shopping mall for their daily walk. They are allowed to enter an hour and a half before the stores are opened for business.

It's wonderful for the walkers. They feel very safe with the uniformed security guards in evidence, as well as comfortable with the climate-controlled building. It's warm in the winter and cool in the summer.

These older adults realize that walking is good exercise and great for their well being. Many have had health problems, and their doctors have recommended walking to them.

Occasionally, professionals sponsored by various medical organizations are on hand to check blood pressure, cholesterol and other health matters.

The mall was designed with businesses on each side of a large aisle including a big department store on one end and a food court at the other end. There are two wide aisles throughout with freestanding kiosks dividing them. The food court is considered the headquarters by the walkers. It is where they meet, leave their belongings and have their refreshments after their exercise.

One of the coffee establishments sells a permanent mug to the senior citizens who can fill it up each day for 50 cents, except on Monday when there is no charge. The offer is good until opening time when the prices return to normal.

You can tell the "regulars" sporting their coffee mugs as they saunter along the walkways .

The traffic is not controlled, but everyone walks to the aisle on the right. The entire trip is one-third of a mile. In order to keep an accurate count, some place a specific number of coins in one hand and deposit one in a pocket each time they cross the starting point. That way, they can keep a correct

Mall Walk

number of how far they have walked, as long as they don't forget to switch that coin when they pass the starting line.

Everyone has a separate personality and the walkers are no exception. Some walk very slowly due to their health or age, some keep up a normal pace, and some move so fast it seems as if they're running. One of the fast steppers always makes a sound reminiscent of the old automobile horns that go "ooga, ooga" as he approaches from the rear. It never fails to bring a smile to those he passes by.

Then, there is an older gentleman who is referred to as the bionic man. He has had both knees and hips replaced and extensive surgery done on one shoulder. He maintains a normal stride and completes three miles every day. He is considered a hero.

They're a very interesting group. Seniors have been around for a long time and have experienced and seen many events and changes in the world. They reminisce, discuss current world and local news and talk about their health.

It's wonderful to hear about the good old days and how these people were involved. How different things were when they were young. Compared to today, they were the good old days for sure.

There are some people who walk very little or not at all. They congregate at a table in the food

Funny Bone

court and enjoyed each other's company with their coffee.

Still, there are others who share the morning newspaper to solve the two crossword puzzles. One is easy, the other, hard. With five or six heads together, both puzzles are resolved in due course.

One day a local television station sent a reporter and a cameraman to the mall before the stores opened. No one knew why they were there, but there was much speculation that they were doing a program on the walkers. Otherwise, why would they be there at such an early hour? The reporter stopped one of the regulars, who thought that he was going to be interviewed and would be on television. Instead, the reporter was interested in the timer device that the walker was wearing around his neck. He laughed about the incident when he told everyone about it.

Their health discussions are serious, but sometimes they can be funny. One such incident was a conversation with a lady regarding the open-heart surgery she had undergone earlier.

She was doing fine and walking two miles every day. When she had her operation, the doctor replaced a part of her heart with a pig's valve.

She said that she didn't eat bacon or sausage for three years since she thought she might be eating her sister.

And she was serious.

Jack, the Boss

Guy Dunn was an avid hunter. Even though he worked at a building supply company for most of his life, his heart was with his hunting dogs. He even turned down invitations that would force him to leave town and his dogs. He might take a quick trip to one of the nearby universities for a football or basketball game, but that was it.

Everyone who knew Guy also were well aware that his hunting dogs were the most important things in his life. He talked about them as if they were his children. Guy was a bachelor so in some regard, they were his family.

At his home, Guy had built an elaborate kennel in his backyard. The enclosure was totally fenced in containing a heated shelter with running water. It was a state of the art project for its time. Since Guy worked for a building supply firm, he was in a good position to go first class.

Guy had a girl friend named Brilla. They had been going together since high school and had never gotten married. Brilla lived with her father and mother and Guy lived in the home he inherited from his parents. They were considered a couple by many of their friends. Whenever someone invited them to a function, it was always as Guy and Brilla. No one ever asked Guy or Brilla to bring a date. It was assumed that they would come together. It never seemed to bother either of them as much as it did Brilla's family. They thought the two should be married. Their romance had been going on long enough and neither was getting any younger.

People felt sorry for Brilla. She had a good job at the local bank, but they thought she was wasting her life with Guy. It was time for her to settle down and raise a family.

Of children, not dogs.

Many thought that Guy was happier with his

Jack, the Boss

dogs than he was with Brilla. Others thought that maybe Brilla had no great fondness for dogs, particularly hunting dogs. She had two beautiful cats herself. Everybody knows that dogs and cats do not make the best of friends

Regardless of what people thought, Guy and Brilla still were an item. When Guy was not hunting, the two of them were together.

Guy never allowed any of the dogs in his home. He felt that their kennel was just as good as his house. During his mother's lifetime, no dogs were allowed in her home. The rule was still enforced after her death.

The highest honor one could receive from Guy was to have a dog named for them. It may have seemed silly or unimportant, but to the master, it was the ultimate tribute. He had named several of his pack for people with whom he worked including his boss, Jack. Jack, the boss, and Jack, the dog.

Then, there were Henry, Al, Otto, Billy, Judy, and Maxine. All of the honorees were his friends; the named animals, his family. Most people were delighted to have a namesake, even if it was a dog. Occasionally, some even bought presents for the hounds. Others would visit them from time to time. Knowing how much it meant to Guy, they played the game.

One Monday morning when Guy went to work

Funny Bone

his boss, Jack, was sick and was staying at home. By Wednesday, Jack was still ailing and not back at the company. A customer came in and inquired, "How's Jack today?"

Guy thought about it for a moment before answering, "He's fatter than a hog and got no hair on his tail."

The customer was surprised. He looked at Guy, frowned and scratched his head.

Jack, the dog, and Jack, the boss.

Sun Roof

My daughter Mary married an Italian. A real Italian. Not an American-Italian, but a genuine pasta eating, wine drinking, fun loving Italian. They met in a French class they both were attending in Paris. He couldn't speak English, and she couldn't speak Italian. As they got to know each other better, they started dating, speaking only in French to one another. As time passed, he picked up a few English phrases. Not to be outdone, she learned some Italian expressions, but their conversations were still predominantly in French. It was a unique situation. Here were two people living in a foreign country with neither speaking his nor her own native tongue.

As the romance blossomed, each began to study the other's language and tried to communicate with it. He spoke English to her, she responded in Italian to him. When they ran into a problem understanding the other, they reverted to French. In any case, they were able to work out the language barrier.

After more than a year of courtship, they were married. My new Italian son-in-law had been working for three years for an insurance company in Italy, and had been sent to their Paris office. While in France, he had enrolled in the French class where he had met my daughter. After their wedding, he was transferred back to the office in Milan

A few years later, they had a son and named him Andrea (Andrew in English) after his deceased Italian grandfather. By that time, Mary and her husband were equally fluent in each other's language. The new father spoke Italian to his son, the new mother, English.

When Andrea began to talk, he was bilingual. He would rattle off English to his *mama'* and Italian to his *papa'*. It was spellbinding to hear this child understanding and communicating in both languages at the same time.

When Mary and her family visited us in the U.S. for a few months to have extensive dental work done, she came with 5-year old Andrea. My little Italian-American grandson was captivated by American television. He sat by the set completely mesmerized. The situation grew tense at mealtime when he didn't want to eat until the program he was watching ended. We had to plan our meals on the hour or half hour to keep him happy. Without a doubt, his English improved immensely within a short time. He mimicked a number of cartoon characters which worried his mother. Familiar phrases spoken by a variety of television animals were ringing in our ears. Whenever Andrea spoke in Italian, his mother would insist, "Speak English, speak English."

She was anxious for him to be completely immersed in English during his visit. After a month, he spoke very little Italian. When his father telephoned from Italy and spoke to him, he spoke Italian. When he turned to his mother and continued to speak in his father's tongue, Mary would insist, "Andrea, speak English, speak English."

Eventually, my son-in-law came for a two-week vacation before accompanying his family back to Italy. He was anxious to see New York City and

Funny Bone

visit some cousins in New Jersey. He and my daughter decided to leave Andrea with my wife and me for a few days. Every now and then, Andrea would ask questions about his parents, sometimes in Italian, sometimes in English. When he fretted in Italian, I reminded him, "Speak English, speak English." He usually would smile and say, "I forgot." I explained to him that we were not playing a game, but trying to teach him to speak and understand English better.

When his parents were returning from their trip, he wanted to go with me to the airport to meet them. He could hardly go to sleep the night before their arrival due to his excitement.

We were driving to the airport for the homecoming when he asked me in English to open the sunroof of my car. It was a beautiful day and the air would feel good. I knew the Italian word for sun (*sole*) and for roof (*tetto*). *Sole tetto.* Was that the way it was referred to in Italy.

I asked Andrea, "How do you say "sun roof" in Italian?"

Looking at me with suspicion, he responded, "Speak English, speak English."

Pen Set

When I first started out in the real estate business in the 1950's, I went to work for an old family firm which had been founded in the early 1920's. It was not my family and there was no personal connection between us, only from a professional standpoint.

Before joining them, I had been working for a bank since finishing college. I had always been interested in real estate and had taken a course in night school in order to get my salesman license which was a requirement by the state. When an opening came up in their company, I applied for the job and got it.

The grandfather who had founded the firm specialized in the sales, leasing and management of commercial and industrial properties. When his two sons joined him before World War II, the firm grew fast and became very successful and prominent in the city.

After the war, the grandfather died and the two sons continued to run the business. Because of the post-war economy, they jumped into the development boom, promoting housing projects, office buildings and shopping centers. In the meantime, one of the brothers brought his young son into the office after he had graduated from college.

The two brothers who were the second generation in the firm ran the company as co-equals. It was definitely managed by both. No important decisions were made by one without the approval of the other.

The brothers shared the same business philosophy but were two distinct personalities. The older was more outgoing, fun loving and charming. The younger was serious, reserved and sharp. It didn't take me too long to adjust to their two styles and temperaments. Even though each was dedicated to his work, their methods of solving problems and accomplishing their goals were completely different.

I thought maybe this was the reason that they got along so well together. There was no sibling rivalry between them. In fact, they respected one another and realized each other's strong points and weaknesses.

When I wanted to take a few days off, I always approached the older man. He was more understanding and sympathetic. When I needed some real estate guidance and advice, I usually contacted the younger brother. He had a steel trap of a mind and could zero in on any situation. Understanding both of them made the system work out very well for me.

My job was in property management for which I was paid a salary and was expected to devote 75% of my time. The remaining 25% was used for property sales for which I earned a commission. Weekends were my own and it was up to me to decide whether or not to push the selling part. In the house selling business, weekends were very important. That's the time working people are available and looking at properties.

There were other employees with the company. In addition to the receptionist, secretaries and bookkeeper, there were two other salesmen, the owners, the son and me. I worked closely with the entire staff, learning the fundamentals of residential and commercial real estate, selling, leasing and management. Their long time experience in all aspects of the business gave me a wonderful opportunity to acquire knowledge which is not generally found in school textbooks. Everyone was very helpful, knowing that I was new to the field and eager to learn as much as I could.

The number one son of the company became interested in the appraisal part of the business, taking various courses to obtain his professional appraisal designation, which he eventually received. He was closer to my age than the others so we ended up becoming very good friends in addition to supporting each other in our separate endeavors.

My two bosses and the son had the fanciest offices and deluxe equipment. Since they owned the business, it was fair and proper. The rest of the staff dreamed of one day having a private office as nice as theirs. We knew that if we were ever going to succeed in that regard, we had to work for it ourselves.

In my job, many people came into the office to see me about aspects of the property they were renting through the firm. Many times, leases or renewals were signed at my desk. Checks were

Pen Set

written for rent payments. Rent applications and written comments or complaints were filed. Many times, my personal fountain pen was used. There was no desk set, including a pen, available. I thought that I should have one.

In those days before ballpoint pens, a fountain pen was used. They were the kind that were filled with ink. I confronted the older brother to see if the company would provide one for me. He agreed that it should.

He instructed me to go to the office supply store a few doors away and pick out an appropriate desk set. Charge it to the company account. He further suggested that I choose a pen with a medium point, not a blunt or fine one. A medium point. In that way, if I ever left their employ, the next rental manager would be able to use the same pen. A person who preferred a fine point would more than likely settle for a medium point . Conversely, one who preferred a blunt point would settle for a medium one.

I felt great. I had been detailed to make my own decision in purchasing a medium point desk set. It would be my own decision as to what it looked like and how much it would cost. As I walked toward the door, I thought that I wouldn't get the most expensive one nor the cheapest. Somewhere in-between would be the best choice. It should be a nice one since it would be used in a business

Funny Bone

setting. Customers would expect it to be appropiate for a real estate office.

When I opened the door to leave, the older brother held up his arm and waved me to stop, saying "By the way, don't spend more than a dollar for the set."

"A dollar?" I asked.

"Right. One dollar."

He wasn't joking.

The Sheriff

Chester Wallace was the sheriff of a rural county not too many miles from the state capital. He, his wife and children lived in a small town of approximately 3,500 residents. Chester, whom many called "Chet" or "Sheriff" loved his job and took great pride in it.

Being Sheriff was what was know in Virginia as a constitutional office, meaning that the person had to be elected by the popular vote of the people. It was not an appointed position. The candidate for the office had to win the election in order to become sheriff.

Chet was a large man and in great physical shape. No fat on his bones. He was proud of his physical prowess and would let you know that no one could subdue him. He was ready, willing and able to defend himself

Chet was a great believer that everyone should obey the law. It made no difference to him what a person's station in life was. He treated everyone equally.

Before he decided to run for sheriff, he had become a state highway law enforcement officer, commonly called a "state trooper". He spent twelve years in that capacity until the sheriff in his home area planned to retire. They had worked together on numerous occasions and had become good friends. The retiring sheriff encouraged Chet to run for his office and promised his unconditional support

Chet talked it over with his family, citing the pros and cons of the job in case he was elected. They were all enthusiastic and realized the demands and activity that would be placed on him. He announced his intention to run and no one opposed him. One other person had talked about running, but ruled against it after he found out about Chet. In fact, the would-be candidate called

The Sheriff

Chet to say that he was supporting him

The first arrest made after the swearing in ceremony was the very next night. Being a former state trooper, Chet was keenly aware of speeding automobiles. It was a natural instinct. A fancy sports car zoomed through the downtown main street around 10:30 p.m. Chet figured it was traveling at least thirty miles over the speed limit. He chased the car and clocked it doing two miles per hour more than he had estimated. He turned on his flashing lights and siren and stopped the speedster.

When the sheriff asked to see the license of the driver, the young man replied,

"You don't know who I am, but my father is in the state senate and my godfather is a judge."

Chet interrupted, "Sir, let me see your license, please."

The driver continued, "You didn't understand me. I said that my father is in the state senate, and my...."

Before he could finish, Chet interrupted again, "That's fine. You were exceeding the speed limit by thirty two miles and that's considered reckless driving."

The young driver insisted, "I don't think you understand who I am."

"Do you know who Chester Wallace is? quizzed the somewhat irritated Chet.

"Chester Wallace? I don't think I know him."

"Well, he's the sheriff who is going to give you a ticket for reckless driving. And, if you give him any more lip, he's going to hold you in jail until somebody famous comes to get you out."

The speedster's attitude changed and he cooperated fully, showing his driver's license.

After a year in office, Chet met with a woman who had worked part-time for his family. She came to the sheriff's office, distraught that her nineteen year old son had been arrested and was being held on murder charges. She pleaded with Chet to help her. She knew that her son Arthur was innocent. Chet told her he would look into it and talk with Arthur.

A trial date was set. The sheriff was not involved in the case, but he wanted to attend the hearing if only to give moral support to the accused's mother.

The prosecuting attorney in the case, Lee Kessler, was holding a grudge against Chet. The attorney's wife had failed to attach her county license decal to her automobile. She had been advised twice by one the sheriff's deputies that her old license had expired and she was in violation of the law. Chet felt that two warnings were enough and instructed the deputies to give her a citation if she continued to ignore the law.

There was no third time. A ticket was given to

The Sheriff

Kessler's wife. Chet felt that it was deserved under the circumstances. She was told two times and it was a bad image for the town's attorney and his wife to ignore the law. It was a very bad example.

At Arthur's trial, Chet sat in the spectator's section with the family. Before the court was called to order, Attorney Lee Kessler walked over and shook hands with the sheriff. Niceties were exchanged between the two smiling men.

When Arthur took the stand, Kessler interrogated him, asking, "Arthur, do you know Sheriff Wallace?

"Yes, sir.

Kessler continued, "Your mother works sometimes for Mrs. Wallace, right?

"Yes, sir.

"And your mother asked Sheriff Wallace to talk with you when you were charged with murder. Is that right?"

"Yes, sir."

Kessler looked around at the jury with a smirk on his face, nodding his head up and down. "And, Sheriff Wallace told you what to say when you were on trial, didn't he?"

Arthur answered, "That's correct, sir."

Kessler removed his glasses, and with one hand pointing at the jury, dramatically raised his voice. "Arthur, tell me and the jury exactly what Sheriff Wallace told you to say."

Kessler was smirking, still shaking his head up and down, thinking he had exposed Chet as fixing the trial.

A moment passed before Arthur spoke, "Sheriff Wallace told me one thing," he paused.

"He told me to tell the truth."

Sheriff Chester Wallace sat there with the biggest smile on his face.

You Can't Win

It's a known fact that children are always getting the best of their parents. It starts the very day they're born and lasts a lifetime. Fathers and mothers learn early that they can never win, no matter how hard they try.

My younger son Bill was attending college that was located in a rural Virginia setting about ten miles from a small town. He and his friends referred to it as out in the boonies. I thought it was not only a wonderful first-rate school but also an ideal place to get an education since there would be few distractions to keep one from studying. At lease, that what I thought when he decided to go there.

I was shocked when Bill came home in late spring after his sophomore year with the startling news that he had flunked his second semester French class. He had been an all round good student throughout high school as well as during his college freshman year.

"We're going back to school and see your French teacher. And I mean today. Get in the car," I ordered.

I made my son telephone ahead and make an appointment with the professor for us that very afternoon.

Bill tried to talk me out of going. He was upset not only with his poor performance in French but also concerned about his plans for the summer. He had gotten a temporary job at Virginia Beach and had rented an apartment there with three of his buddies. He had also paid his part of the security deposit and his share of the first month's rent.

He didn't like it when I even hinted that he might have to postpone his beach trip and possibly go to summer school. In addition, he would probably lose his job there.

As we drove to the college, we discussed his situation. We bounced back and forth while riding. What was the reason he failed? Was the language class too difficult for him? Did he have any indication during the term that he was failing? Was his teacher too demanding? Did he study enough?

He informed me that he had made an "A" in the course during the first semester.

I could not understand why he did so badly during the second term.

"Did you miss a lot of classes?" I asked.

"I think I missed only three during the semester," he responded.

Then, I started with my sermon about the family having to make sacrifices to be able to send him and his brother and sisters to college. We did not have a money tree. I had to work long and hard to be able to afford it. I had four children to educate. His mother and I looked at it as an investment in their future and we took it very seriously. It cost a great deal to get an education and neither of us expected him to fail.

When we arrived for our appointment at the college, I was somewhat surprised to see this rather young looking military type guy in a leather jacket and helmet drive up on his motorcycle. My son commented that his teacher had a doctorate in French and had been a Green Beret soldier in the

Vietnam War. He looked like a no nonsense and gung-ho individual, and I wondered if maybe Bill was a bit afraid of him.

After we all exchanged pleasantries, I was told that my son was capable of doing well in the course but had gradually lost interest in it.

During further discussion, I informed the professor that my son had told me he had only missed three classes during the term.

The teacher shook his head, looked at Bill and asked, "Did you forget to tell your father that two of those three absences were the mid-term and the final exam?"

I got the picture.

Bill was sent to summer school.

He completed the course in a matter of a few weeks, receiving an "A" in it and being exempt from taking the final exam. He later told me that there was nothing to do on campus during the summer months except to study.

He made it to the beach a little late and had worked something out with his employers for his temporary job there.

Everything worked out for him in the end, but I couldn't help thinking about those three classes he missed.

You just can't win.

A couple years later during his senior year, Bill served as president of his fraternity. He lived in the house with several other members. I would telephone him every now and then to see how he was doing and to keep him up to date on family news.

At that time, his hair was a bit on the long side, not to his shoulders, but shaggy looking. His friends nicknamed him "Shag" because of it. No one in our family ever called him anything but "Bill". None of his friends called him anything but "Shag".

Whenever I telephoned the fraternity house and asked for "Bill" rather than "Shag", his friends were automatically alerted by the name. Over a period of time, they began to recognize my voice. Sometimes, he would be there, but at other times he would not be in his room. They waited a few minutes before telling me that "Bill" was not in, but at the library.

I was impressed that my son was studying so hard. Maybe he had learned a good lesson from flunking that French class when he was a sophomore. I knew it was difficult to concentrate at the fraternity house with all the many interruptions and noisy activity there. I thought it was smart of him to go to the library where it was quiet and conducive to studying.

It was not until later that I found out I was being outwitted again.

My wife and I attended parents' day at the

college. As we drove through the small town nearby, we stopped for a traffic signal. While waiting for the light to turn green, I looked over at some of the store buildings. My eyes focused on an establishment that was an obvious beer joint whose sign read, "The Library".

Ah, ha! So that's the Library those college kids were telling me about when I called my son.

"Bill" was always at the Library.

You just can't win.

Order Form for
Funny Bone

Please send to:

Name:_____

Street/Box _____ Apt____

City_____ State____Zip_____

Include Check or Money Order to:

> Five Star Press
> P. O. Box 8454
> Richmond, VA
> 23226

_____copies @$19.95 each _____

VA residents add 4.5% sales tax ($.90 ea.)_____

Shipping & handling (per copy) _____ 2.50

Total. . . . . ._____